"Anyone engaged in constructing a contemporary Jewish theology must proceed carefully so as not to try to shove the square pegs of modern thought and experience into the cylindrical holes of classical Jewish life and thinking. Nevertheless, an awareness of all these challenges should not discourage the project and progress of Jewish theology, but rather serve to mark the path along which the journey should proceed. It is not an easy or identifiable road. Flipping through the pages of this book, you will readily see that we live in an age when the boundaries of what constitutes Jewish theological thought are as wide as they are sometimes imperceptible."

—FROM THE INTRODUCTION

From the Garden of Eden onward, the God-idea has taken on a varied and ever-evolving number of expressions within Judaism. From Mount Sinai to the prophets of the exile, from Maimonides' *Guide for the Perplexed* to Kabbalah, from Chasidism to mid-twentieth-century North America, theological inquiry, diverse in its content and idiom, has sustained the Jewish People.

The passionate voices of a new generation of Jewish thinkers continue that dialogue with God, examining the dynamics of what Jews can believe today. They explore:

- A dynamic God in process
- The canon of Jewish literature and its potential to be both contemporary and authentic to tradition
- Critical terms and categories for discussing Jewish theology
- The ongoing nature of the Jewish search for God
- Ruptures within the modern Jewish condition
- And much more

"Demonstrates ... that there is a future to the Jewish theological enterprise.... A superb text for a theology discussion group or adult education class."

—*CJ: Voices of Conservative/Masorti Judaism*

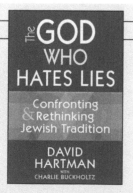

JEWISH THEOLOGY IN OUR TIME

A New Generation Explores the Foundations and Future of Jewish Belief

EDITED BY RABBI ELLIOT J. COSGROVE, PhD

FOREWORD BY RABBI DAVID J. WOLPE

PREFACE BY RABBI CAROLE B. BALIN, PhD

For People of All Faiths, All Backgrounds
JEWISH LIGHTS Publishing

Jewish Theology in Our Time:
A New Generation Explores the Foundations and Future of Jewish Belief

2013 Quality Paperback Edition, First Printing

Library of Congress Cataloging-in-Publication Data
Jewish theology in our time : a new generation explores the foundations and future of Jewish belief / edited by Elliot J. Cosgrove.
p. cm.
Includes bibliographical references.
ISBN-13: 978-1-58023-413-9
ISBN-10: 1-58023-413-5
1. Judaism—Doctrines. 2. God (Judaism) I. Cosgrove, Elliot J.
BM602.J49 2010
296.3—dc22
2010009313

ISBN: 978-1-58023-630-0 (paperback)

Manufactured in the United States of America
Cover Design: Jenny Buono
Cover Art: Shraga Weil, "Heritage II," signed and numbered serigraph published by Safrai Gallery, Jerusalem, Israel; www.safrai.com.

Published by Jewish Lights Publishing

To my favorite new voices in Jewish life, my children:
Lucy, Madeline, Zoe, and Jed

May each of you one day share the faith
expressed first by the Israelites at the Red Sea:

This is my God, and I will glorify Him;
My father's God, and I will exalt Him
—Exodus 15:2

Contents

THE GOD IN PROCESS

THE GODS OF THE TEXT

Contents

WAYS OF TALKING ABOUT GOD

A QUEST FOR GOD

THE GOD IN BETWEEN

Foreword

Rabbi David J. Wolpe

THE JEWISH PEOPLE, Abraham Joshua Heschel famously declared, is a messenger that has forgotten its message. In the intervening years, the dilemma has become more acute: we are a people that has largely forgotten that we have a mission.

Theology is about the restoration of mission as well as the clarification of message. "This is what I believe"—that is the marching order of a theological statement. Though couched in complexity, qualification, textual nuance, and sometimes (we hope!) elegant prose, the theologian offers a booster shot of belief. In the tangle of life circumstance and changing mores, where can a modern Jew stand confident in his or her faith, in his or her Torah?

There were times when Torah did battle with a single, unified ideological opponent: Torah versus Christianity, or Islam, or Aristotle, or the internal rejectionism of the Karaites. But today there are challenges on all fronts: biology, astronomy, comparative religion, sociological study, textual criticism, historical consciousness, and many, many others. As Jews in the modern world, to ignore the proliferation of challenging disciplines is to declare ourselves irrelevant. Embracing the challenges is to recognize the enormity of our task.

Ultimately the thread that binds Jewish teaching together is relationship. The Jew must establish a relationship with God, with self, with other Jews, with the non-Jewish world, with the Land of Israel and even with the marvel of creation. The filament that binds us to each of these will be spun differently in the hands of each thinker. None can be ignored, and the diversity of views you will hear in these pages attests to the many ways in which the task can be understood and undertaken.

The interested reader should keep his or her eye on one more great change in Jewish theology. The modern non-Orthodox theologian need not begin knowing where he or she must end up. The defense of standard halakhic practice is no longer a given. Perhaps she or he will end up with a modified Halakhah, or a stringent version, or none at all. Although governed in some sense by fidelity to the Torah, that fidelity takes all sorts of self-declared forms in the modern age. In addition to theology performing the work of clarifying belief, it is crucial for shaping practice.

Some will find this swirling cauldron an inspiriting joy. Others may find it confusing, even saddening. Why can we not settle on an approach that will bring the Jewish community together, an approach to which we can all subscribe? Alas (or thank God) such was never the case in Jewish history—the unity of the past is vastly exaggerated in the collective memory—and it is even less true today. In a modern, scientifically advancing age, with the State of Israel and the fraught but materially successful diaspora, the People Israel will sing many songs. Some will be discordant; many will not harmonize easily with the others. In this book are the new theological singers of Israel, each adding his or her own individual notes to the grand chorus. There is much here to provoke, disturb, and discomfit you. But you will also find great beauty and depth. We may not agree on the content of the message. How wonderful, however, to be reminded that we are the bearers of an ancient and essential message. How necessary the struggle to give voice to that message. In that struggle is the beginning of wisdom.

PREFACE

RABBI CAROLE B. BALIN, PHD

"YOU'RE TEACHING *WHAT*?" asked a classmate in grad school two decades ago, when she heard I was offering a class at a local synagogue.

"Jewish theology," I repeated, growing slightly impatient with her questions.

"But what do you mean by *that*?" she asked, as her traditional Jewish upbringing slipped into sharp relief against the walls of our university.

It was as if I were speaking in a foreign tongue. Doing Jewish theology—the process of piecing together a personally meaningful understanding of God—was utterly alien to her. In her religious life, she was accustomed to speaking exclusively to, and not necessarily about, the Divine.

For sure, for millennia, Jews have spoken *to* God. Patriarchs and priests, matriarchs and mystics, prophets and poets have "poured out [their] heart[s]" (Psalm 62:9) in the hope of a Reply. We can't blame them for trying. After all, according to the master narrative of Jewish tradition embedded in the Torah, the God of the Israelites did respond to the people at Mt. Sinai, and, apparently, to all descendants to follow. Given that stunning revelation, it didn't take long for Jews to start talking *about* God. Indeed, God-talk has wended its way through time and space, leaving in its wake countless attempts by Jews to apprehend, comprehend, and contend with essential questions relating to the Divine.

The nub of the matter for the historian of religion is the extent to which Jews of any given era permitted outside influences to infringe upon their distinctive thought and way of life. Philo of Alexandria (20–50 CE) is generally regarded as the first post-biblical Jew to step boldly and self-consciously beyond the boundaries of Jewish learning in a quest to understand God. He relieved his rationalist discomfort with biblical passages that ascribed human-like qualities to the Divine (i.e., anthropomorphism) by importing the Hellenistic hermeneutic of allegory into the Jewish world. Others followed him. The medieval period is peppered with the likes of Saadia Gaon and Yehuda Halevi (whose anti-philosophical tract is actually philosophic in form), along with Hasdai Crescas and Joseph Albo. But it is, of course, Rambam's Aristotelian-influenced thought that changed forever the depth and breadth of theological conversation among Jews.

Notwithstanding his persistently powerful influence in our own day, one can safely assume that only a small circle of devotees and critics paid much heed to Rambam's philosophy in his day. Throughout the Middle Ages, the overwhelming majority of ordinary Jews continued to serve God through the daily observance of divine commandments. Practice made perfect, so to speak, rendering belief rather beside the point.

Then the great light of modernity shined down on Jewish men of Western Europe. Clutching in one hand the rights and obligations of citizenship and in the other the promises of progress, they fled the yeshivah for the inner sanctum of the university where they studied history, philology, and philosophy. New understandings of reality opened before them as Romanticism, paleontology, Darwinism, and biblical criticism forced a reassessment of religious assumptions. Rival ideologies splintered modern Jewish communities and led ultimately though unwittingly to the development of religious movements, who looked optimistically toward a future where Jew and gentile would join in common cause to bring about the messiah or its rational equivalent, the messianic era. In the age of Immanuel Kant, Hermann Cohen recast the *categorical imperative* into a systematic Jewish theology known as ethical monotheism. The latter would become a household name in the next century, even as social justice became a raison d'être for many American Jews; and Isaac Luria's sixteenth-century cosmology was unearthed and reshaped into a type of do-goodism known far and wide as *tikkun olam* (repairing the world).

Over the course of the twentieth century, the Jewish theological enterprise exploded. Modernism would eventually cede to postmodernism, a project that challenges and upends rationalist notions of objectivity and truth. But not before Martin Buber's theology of dialogue seduced tens of thousands of God-seekers; Abraham Joshua Heschel turned the quest for God on its head by imagining the Divine in search of us; and Mordecai Kaplan's human-centered, disembodied "Power that makes for salvation" supplanted supernaturalism and brought many quietly agnostic Jews back to God. Gershom Scholem resurrected the Kabbalah of old by bringing his critical mind to bear on its study, forcing a détente of sorts between the age-old rivalry between rationalists and mystics.

Historical events of mid-century, unexpectedly and tragically, deepened theological exploration and contemplation. In the shadow of the Shoah, Emil Fackenheim and Richard Rubenstein, among others, endeavored to make sense (or non-sense) out of the inexplicable. Jewish theologians from Abraham Isaac Kook to Abba Hillel Silver grappled with the fulfillment of the Jewish hope that the Jews would once again be a free people in the Land.

The numbers of those doing theology expanded as the century drew to a close. Rachel Adler, Eliezer Berkovits, Eugene Borowitz, Elliot Dorff, Marcia Falk, Neil Gillman, Arthur Green, Yitz Greenberg, David Hartman, Louis Jacobs, Yeshayahu Leibowitz, Emmanuel Levinas, Judith Plaskow, Zalman Schachter-Shalomi, Joseph Solveitchik, Ellen Umansky, Arthur Waskow, Shneur Zalman, and others established Jewish theology as a foregone conclusion of contemporary Jewish life.

There can be no doubt that of all the constructive influences of the twentieth century, second-wave feminism has brought about the greatest transformation in Jewish theology and life. Women like Judith Plaskow and Rachel Adler challenged the power dynamics of patriarchy that are reified and reinforced even in Judaism's master narrative. Decades ago, feminists cracked open the Pandora's box of theological and liturgical language, arguing that the metaphors we have employed for centuries had lost their currency and power, and serve to alienate rather than welcome. The nearly two hundred female contributors to *The Torah: A Women's Commentary*, edited by Tamara Eskenazi and Andrea Weiss, will go a long way in correcting that imbalance. Feminists have also questioned the transcendent model of God, championing instead an imminent one that favors connection. More recently, postmodernists have questioned the very categories of male and female, leading us to puzzle anew the meaning of "male and female God created them" (Genesis 1:27).

Pondering God's nature and our relationship to the Divine is no longer the purview of scholars alone. In a society where debates about creationism and evolution rage in newspaper headlines and beliefs about God inform national policy, to engage in this conversation makes us de facto theologians.

The theological impulse has even seeped into contemporary American pop culture. Kabbalah has sprouted in strange and unexpected places (like Hollywood). Eastern religious thought and practice has moved westward. And, most recently, environmental concerns have inspired a new generation to become attuned to God's wondrous but despoiled earth.

It is clear from this survey that God-talk has crept from the periphery toward the center of Jewish conversation. It is my fervent hope that more Jews will come forward to talk the talk. Like the editor of this worthy volume, I am troubled by the shortage of women and Orthodox Jews who responded affirmatively to his invitation to make a mark on these pages. As the twenty-first century unfolds, I hope we will make good on the promise captured in the title of Tamar Ross' *Expanding the Palace of Torah*, the newest addition to the Jewish theological canon.

To the essayists who boldly tread a religious path and added their words to the growing theological compendium of Jewish life, this God-seeker is grateful.

INTRODUCTION

"To this day, there is no intellectually formulated conception
which has acquired authoritative recognition in Judaism as
the only true idea of God. The inevitable conclusion to which
we are led by the consideration of the God-idea in the history
of the Jewish People, and of the part played by it in civilization in general, is that the Jewish civilization cannot survive
without the God-idea as an integral part of it, but it is in no
need of having any specific formulation of that idea authoritative for all Jews."

—MORDECAI KAPLAN, *JUDAISM AS CIVILIZATION*[1]

THIS VOLUME ARRIVES by way of the two assumptions embedded in
Mordecai Kaplan's insight. First, for Judaism to claim both authenticity
and viability, a grappling with God—in other words, theology—has
been a necessary element of that Judaism. Second, and perhaps equally
controversial, is that from the Garden of Eden onward, the God-idea
has taken on a varied and ever-evolving number of expressions. From
Mount Sinai to the prophets of the exile, from Maimonides' *Guide for
the Perplexed* to Kabbalah, from Chasidism to mid-twentieth-century
North America, theological inquiry, diverse in its content and idiom,
has sustained the Jewish People. This book represents an effort to continue that Jewish dialogue with God into the future.

Why Is Theology Important?

Perhaps the most succinct answer to this question was provided by the
late Jewish scholar and activist Arthur Hertzberg, who explained, "A

community cannot survive on what it remembers; it will persist only because of what it affirms and believes."[2] When *kashrut* is practiced without a theological matrix in place, it is a form of dietary cliquishness, not a distinguishing and distinctive expression of commandedness. When circumcision is practiced without an understanding of covenant, it is not a sign of a sacrosanct relationship with God, but a primitive if not objectionable rite. If commitment to Israel is framed solely in political terms, the argument for a modern state becomes less and less compelling for American Jews, Israelis, and, for that matter, everyone else. Theological inquiry has sustained the Jewish People. Without it, Judaism becomes a dry, brittle, and lifeless artifact.

A theologian is entrusted with the task of theorizing on the nature of God. Unlike the academic studying ancient religion, the theologian, as my teacher Rabbi Louis Jacobs taught, must ask what it is that one can believe *today*. There is a deeply personal element to theology in that it both emerges out of our experiences and seeks to speak to them. Theological thought is both a partisan and a constructive project. Yet, in this very claim lies the rub. For while seeking to describe an eternal and unchanging God, theology inevitably reflects the thoughts of a particular generation or person. How can God's singular and immutable nature be subject to the diversity and whims of humankind? The theologian's task is made more difficult in the realization that knowledge of God is necessarily beyond the capacity of human discourse. As the fifteenth-century theologian Joseph Albo put it, "*If I knew God, I would be God.*"[3] The non-fundamentalist theologian seeks to describe what she or he knows, from the start, cannot be described. Theological integrity thus also requires humility. Even as one seeks God's nearness, God's presence remains ever high and hidden.

The Jewish theologian is faced with the additional task of constructing a theology emergent from and tethered to Jewish sources, people, and concerns. Jewish theology must be identifiable with Jewish thinkers of the past and also find traction with Jews of the present. A theology that fails to meet the first criterion, while potentially interesting, risks faddishness and cannot rightfully claim to be Jewish. A theology that doesn't meet the second criterion, while claiming authenticity, is irrelevant.

Finally, the Jewish theologian builds on a tradition that is neither univocal nor systematic. Any student of the Jewish tradition knows well that the canon of Jewish literature expresses itself in an organic and pluralistic fashion. With notable exceptions (Maimonides, Albo, Crescas), Jewish thought is more aptly described as a "concentration of many ideas and ideals"[4] than as any single dogma or doctrinal creed. Furthermore, there is a gap between what constitutes contemporary Western theological or philosophical discourse and indigenous modes of biblical and rabbinic thinking. Again, in the words of my teacher Rabbi Louis Jacobs, the Rabbis were "not inferior philosophers, they were not bad philosophers or philosophers without an adequate philosophic training. They were not philosophers at all."[5] Anyone engaged in constructing a contemporary Jewish theology must proceed carefully so as not to try to shove the square pegs of modern thought and experience into the cylindrical holes of classical Jewish life and thinking. Nevertheless, an awareness of all these challenges should not discourage the project and progress of Jewish theology, but rather serve to mark the path along which the journey should proceed. It is not an easy or identifiable road. Flipping through the pages of this book, you will readily see that we live in an age when the boundaries of what constitutes Jewish theological thought are as wide as they are sometimes imperceptible.

With the above considerations in mind, you face the altogether reasonable question of how Jewish theology may be read and evaluated. If Jewish theology is internally pluralistic, deeply personal, and necessarily incomplete, then how do you distinguish good Jewish theology from bad Jewish theology? The present volume claims to signal the state of emerging thought at this present moment. How exactly should you evaluate the merits of the Jewish theology it contains?

To answer this question, I recommend the standards proposed by my teacher Dr. Byron Sherwin. Sherwin offers the following four criteria by which to measure Jewish (or any) theology: authenticity, coherence, contemporaneity, and communal acceptance.

> Authenticity depends upon the nature and use of sources
> consulted and on the faith commitment of the individual
> consulting them. Coherence relates to the cohesion, clarity
> and communicability of a formulated theological perspec-
> tive. Contemporaneity pertains to the successful applica-
> tion of past traditions to present situations. Communal
> acceptance refers to the ratification of a theological posture
> by committed members of a specific faith community.[6]

Sherwin's criteria are significant not so much because they are easily
applied, but rather because they provide a common ground for beginning
a dialogue. Like any art form, theology is subject to aesthetic judgments
occurring across generations. We will all have to wait and see whether or
not any of the voices in this volume find acceptance in generations to
come. Ultimately, the success of any work of theology is in its ability to
stimulate another person toward assessing his or her own beliefs.

Who Are the New Voices in Jewish Theology?

The subtitle of this volume includes the qualifying "New Generation."
The newness of the contributors is defined not so much by chronological
age but by the shared attribute that none have published a major work of
Jewish theology (although I believe all are capable of doing so). There is
a delightfully prospective quality to the voices assembled on these pages.
For each contributor, I believe, his or her best work lies ahead.

In seeking new voices, every effort was made to invite "up and coming" thinkers from across the Jewish spectrum. Invitations were issued
to both rabbis and Jewish academics with an existential stake in the
faith community of Israel (a slippery criterion to be sure). Authors from
North America, Europe, and Israel were asked to contribute, though
the English language requirement inevitably limited the range of contributors (one chapter was translated from its original Hebrew).

Unlike some anthologies on Jewish theology, participants were not
given a non-negotiable punch-list of questions to which they had to
respond. In matters theological, style is substance, and it quickly became

clear that a fixed template would have stifled the thoughts and creativity of the contributors. While I asked a few leading questions (e.g., "Describe your faith as a Jew." "Does the contemporary scene insist on any new questions?"), I did not want to set the terms of discourse too tightly. If you notice a preponderance of concern with some areas (e.g., revelation, theological implications of the State of Israel) and less with others (e.g., theodicy, chosen people), then that fact is itself significant and worthy of discussion. Indeed, if theology is as much about us as about God, then this volume provides a fascinating comment on the perceived concerns confronting the Jewish People today.

Invitations were issued to thinkers affiliated with all streams of Jewish life. Knowing the even-handedness by which invitations were issued, the fact that the overwhelming majority of participants are from the non-Orthodox world raises difficult and pressing questions. Perhaps the most lamentable imbalance of the present volume is the dearth of female voices. Again, having issued an *equal* number of invitations to men and women, I am at a loss to explain this result. It is implausible to me that Jewish women in North America are not interested in Jewish theology. (The three female contributors all reside in Israel). The explanations for these imbalances may be ideological, sociological, interpersonal, stylistic, or a combination of factors. As excited as I am to hear explanations for the imbalances of this volume, I am even more excited to see them corrected in the future. All thought, certainly theological, is enriched and sharpened by being placed in dialogue with other voices. I readily concede the shortcomings of this volume and pray that its deficiencies serve toward inspiring future "more perfect" anthologies.

Nevertheless, one cannot let "perfect" be the enemy of "good." Stuart M. Matlins, the publisher of Jewish Lights, and I were prompted to create this volume for fear that nobody was interested in Jewish theology anymore. We worried that questions of belief were somehow passé and that the "next generation" was not interested in making positive statements about what a Jew can believe today. We have discovered that our fears were unfounded, that passionate new voices are actively engaged in constructing Jewish theology, and that the future of the field is very bright indeed. I hope that this book serves to both reflect the condition of Jewish belief today and identify directions for the future.

A Framework for Dialogue

The task of organizing this anthology is not an easy one. Lacking obvious thematic clusters (e.g., chosenness, revelation, post-Holocaust theology), this book did not lend itself to a readily obvious structure. The decision to create categories is born not so much from an insistence that one particular author must be read in light of another, but rather to enhance the accessibility of the essays and draw out certain shared features in greater relief. Indeed, while not easy, the very project of categorization served as the first step toward assessment, a topic touched on in the Afterword. Namely, what are—if any at all—the shared attributes of this next crop of theologians?

The first section, "The God in Process" (Artson, Fishbane, Held, Jacobson-Maisels, Kalmanofsky), reflects a shared engagement with three interrelated features to differing degrees: an effort to break out of perceived conventional God language toward a notion of a dynamic God in process; a nod to the lexicon and sources of the Chasidic tradition; and by extension, an explicit or implicit engagement with the theological categories of acosmism and panentheism (roughly: "God is the Whole").

The second section, "The Gods of the Text" (Crane, Gordon, Moffic, Rose, Sommer), reflects a sense that the canon of Jewish literature—biblical, rabbinic, and otherwise—bears the potential to be both responsive to the diversity of contemporary theological concerns and authentically anchored in the received traditions.

The third section, "Ways of Talking about God" (Lopatin, Marmur, Plevan, Beit-Halachmi, Shapiro), provides critical terms and categories by which the conversation of Jewish theology can press forward. Each author, leaning on the authority of past thinkers, retrieves, revalorizes, and provides the language that animates their respective theological voices and can be recommended to future efforts.

Each author contained in the fourth section, "A Quest for God" (Cosgrove, Cooper, Morris, Nevins, and Stern), acknowledges the ongoing nature of the Jewish search for God. Whether by prayer, observance of *mitzvot* or devotional study, these authors seek to position the Jewish theological posture as both aspirational and unending.

The authors of the fifth section, "The God in Between" (Elad-Applebaum, Bronstein, Kelman, Sax), seek to reconcile the ruptures embedded within the modern Jewish condition. Each chapter addresses a certain "gap": the gap between the world as is and as idealized in traditional terms, between secular and religious commitments, between traditional and modern worldviews, and otherwise.

As noted, the above categories are tentative at best. Each grouping could easily be reformulated and named according to an alternative organizing principle. Indeed, I encourage you to accept my proposed categories with suspicion, seeking a different structure that will ultimately lead to a better understanding of the features underlying the thought contained in this anthology.

Acknowledgments

My deep thanks go to each contributor for participating in this book. Theological reflection is deeply personal, and I am grateful for your courage in presenting your ideas, allowing them to be sharpened at my clumsy hand and then presented to the public. I am also grateful to the members and leadership of Park Avenue Synagogue, especially my chairman, Steven M. Friedman, and my assistant, Joanne Zablud, for encouraging me to balance my congregational duties with this project. Most of all, I thank Stuart M. Matlins and Emily Wichland of Jewish Lights, without whose encouragement, wisdom, and most of all, patience and faith, this book would never have seen the light of day.

May these essays provoke, kindle, and inspire responses from all those committed to the project of Jewish theology.

THE GOD IN
PROCESS

I Will Be Who I Will Be

A God of Dynamic Becoming

Rabbi Bradley Shavit Artson, DHL

Too often, religion and religious arguments feel coercive—you have to think my way. Let's start by giving permission to think what you think and believe what you believe. My simple hope is to throw a lifeline to people who feel drawn to religion and spirituality, seeking an entrance, while the security guards keep slamming the doors shut. Those are the people I am addressing, offering a little science to help shake up our theology, and to open us to an old/new way of understanding what it means to be in the world, to be alive, and to relate to God.

There are three dogmas that we are told we are supposed to believe about God: that God is all-powerful ("omnipotent"), all-knowing ("omniscient"), and all-good ("omnibenevolent"). These three *omnis* have created more atheists than any cluster of ideas in human history, because God can be any two, but not all three. It is logically impossible to assert that God entails all three, yet theologians have been flinging believers against this logical boundary for a millennium.

Rabbi Bradley Shavit Artson, DHL, (www.bradartson.com) is dean of the Ziegler School of Rabbinic Studies at American Jewish University, where he is vice president. He is author of over two hundred articles and nine books, most recently *The Everyday Torah: Weekly Reflections and Inspirations* (McGraw-Hill). He received his doctorate in philosophy from Hebrew Union College–Jewish Institute of Religion under the supervision of Dr. David Ellenson.

"Omnipotent" means that God has 100 percent of the power—all of it. There are two problems with this claim. The first problem is that power is not an absolute; power reflects relationship. You have to have some power for me to have more than you do. If you have no power whatsoever, then I cannot use any over you because there is no resistance. For the concept of power to mean something, it has to be shared. If God has all the power, and everything else has none, then God has no power either, because a relationship between powers does not exist. The idea of omnipotence consumes itself—a logical self-contradiction.

There is a second problem with omnipotence. If God is truly omnipotent, meaning there is nothing that God cannot do, then it turns out that we are more powerful than God. If God is all-powerful, could God make a weight so heavy that God could not lift it? No, because if it is a weight that God cannot lift, then God is not all-powerful. And if God can't make such a weight, then there's something God can't do. Either way there is something we can do that an all-powerful God cannot. This logic game tells us that this contradiction is no minor problem. There is a difference between saying God is very powerful and saying God is all-powerful. What is the biblical or rabbinic term for all-powerful? It turns out there is no such term or concept.[1] God has g'vurah, g'dullah, koach—synonyms for might and power—but there is no Hebrew for omnipotence. This turns out to be a Greek idea; it derives from Plato and Aristotle.

What about omniscience? When most theologians and clergy use the word all-knowing, they mean that God knows the future precisely as God knows the past. Nothing is hidden from God. There are two problems with this claim: the future has not yet happened and one cannot know something that does not exist. The category of knowing requires existence, unless you believe that everything is predetermined and human freedom is illusory (a decidedly non-biblical and non-rabbinic assertion). So it turns out that thinking about omniscience in terms of God knowing everything in the future is really a way of saying creation is not real. But our tradition insists that creation is real, otherwise God is not really a creator and life is an illusion. There are lots of theologians and traditions making that claim, but no Jewish ones. Even the theologians who think this way do not live their lives as though they really exist. The future will look really different based on our choices, which means, then, that God cannot know the future because we have not decided our part of it yet. And all of the creation, equally real, gets to weigh in on that untrammeled future. God knows absolutely everything possible to know; once an event happens, God knows it forever. But nobody can know what is beyond knowledge, what will become real from the potentials and possibilities the future offers.

Omniscience is a serious problem that becomes insurmountable when linked to omnipotence. If God is all-knowing and all-powerful, then we preserve God's goodness by justifying terrible things happening to innocent people. For example, if God knew that the Holocaust would happen (omniscience), and God could have prevented the Holocaust but chose not to (omnipotence), then it would violate Torah's standards of justice and love to serve that God. A God who could stop a million babies from being murdered and chose not to, for whatever reason, is a monster and a bully. I know that if I saw a baby about to be murdered and I could intervene and stop it, my refraining from action would violate my Torah obligations. Such an abdication does not stop being a monstrosity just because God did it. Torah tradition affirms God's goodness unambiguously and asserts two claims that some theologians do not like to remember: we are told, at the beginning of Genesis, that God gave humans the ability to distinguish between good and evil and that we are made in God's image. That is to say, Torah tells us explicitly that we share the same criteria.

We have philosophical and theological reasons to rethink this problematic theology. There are scientific reasons as well. In the time of Plato and Aristotle, it was believed that the universe is composed of solid substances that interact externally. Forces move objects, the objects interact by bouncing off each other, and the stronger object displaces the weaker. Those metaphysical assumptions explain Newtonian physics and they lead to the dichotomy of dualism: there are two kinds of things, spirits and bodies. Bodies occupy space and time; spirits (or mind) do not. Both substances are real and both are mutually irreducible.

That mind/body split leads to the third and final mystery that religion (and philosophy and science) assumed until the start of the twentieth century: mind (or, if you prefer, soul) is completely non-physical, but it is a substance and it is in the body just the way God is a substance in the universe. God is to universe as spirit is to body. How does something that is completely spiritual impact something that is only physical? If spirit is purely spirit, then how does it lift an arm? What is the connection between spiritual and physical? No philosopher, no scientist, no theologian has ever come up with an answer for that conundrum because there is none.

The possibility of seeing the rich depth of Torah without the distorting sheen of Greek metaphysics and the contemporary solution to our body/mind problem (and the problem of the three *omnis*) starts one hundred and fifty years ago with the publication of Charles Darwin's *Origin of Species*. Darwinian evolution is an idea that has continued to grow ever since it was first articulated to explain the diversity and unity of living things and now explains the cosmos's unity and diversity. Darwinian evolution shows that every living creature is related to every living creature. We all share common ancestry, common genetics, and a common cellular basis for the way we have adapted to life on the earth. There is continuity from the very first living organisms until today. New properties emerge, but they emerge continuously. So we are linked to the creatures that our ancestors were; they are linked to the creatures their ancestors were.

One reason that the Darwinian idea scares some religious people, even though it has overwhelming empirical support, is that it makes it very hard to believe in a force outside of nature who suspends the rules, because evolution provides evidence that creation self-evolves. There is no need for someone intervening. In fact, the system has never shown signs of a break. Ever. What drives this evolutionary process forward is the relentless struggle for survival. There are not enough resources to go around, so we are all clawing our way to get our share of the resources. The driving force of this survival is natural selection, by which classical Darwinians mean that some mutations will be beneficial (you cannot know in advance what they are), and some of them will not, and they will make possible progeny who will replicate that mutation. But it turns out that in the last fifty years, we have recognized that natural selection also means choice and agency. Creatures have a say in their own evolution, in their own choices, in their own development. Some particular fish had to decide to get that bug even though it meant venturing on land. Some fish took a risk and some fish swam away. A particular group of apes had to risk the savanna while others chose the safety of the forest.

Einstein's theory of relativity also helped clear the deck. Einstein reasoned that measurements are always from the perspective of the particular viewer and physics is the same everywhere. The physics on earth is the same physics as a galaxy one hundred billion light years away. What complicates that uniformity is the seemingly innocuous constant, the speed of light. Because light is constant regardless of the perspective of the observer, it poses a limit to relativity that overturns all our common-sense perceptions. Time dilation, spacetime, relativity of simultaneity, mass-energy equivalence all result from this shift of perceptions.

And then the final change in our worldview came through quantum mechanics. Quantum mechanics is the science of the very, very, very, very small. At that level, nothing follows what humans label as logic. Events that have no connection with each other continue to influence each other's behavioral choices. Rather than going around or through a wall, electrons just appear on the far side. Strange constraints in quantum mechanics preclude the possibility of prediction and certainty. Quantum events are probability patterns—there are no solid objects, only packets of energy, of probability.

The Judaism that we have inherited is not just from scripture and rabbinics, but for a thousand years it has been filtered through Greek philosophies that transformed Judaism from an organism of living stories and laws into a supposedly objective description. But Torah never

7

stands outside the story to impose what it means objectively. The Talmud never rules on the metaphysics that its laws instantiate. What Jewish sources invite is a life of engagement: of telling, of *mitzvot*, of refraining from *aveirot* (sins), and of living in covenant. We have been reading Torah through Greek metaphysics, and more recently, we have been reading it through Newtonian physics and Cartesian metaphysics—that split of body and soul—trying to distill some objective essence as though doing, telling, and living weren't enough. We have sold our living birthright for a bowl of Greek porridge. Cartesian metaphysics and Aristotelian and Newtonian sciences are no longer commanding. We are finally free to look at our own Jewish sources without their distorting overlaying.

God is not the exception to the rules; God is the greatest exemplar of the rules. God is not, as Aristotle claimed, the unmoved mover. God is the most moved mover. God is that force in the cosmos generating creativity and novelty. Our universe continuously blossoms into new, more complex interrelationships! These creations are not merely related externally. If you really think about yourself for a moment, you recognize that at a quantum level, you are packets of vibrating energy. Those packets of energy do not change when they are in you and when they are in a chair, or when they are in the air. They remain the same packets of energy, just vibrating all around, but they coalesce as recurrent patterns that we at perceive as stable. As a fetus, you were part of a metabolizing unity including your mother, and that taking in and giving out has never stopped. We are not autonomous substances. Rather, we are interconnected, dynamic events. In fact, everything is in the process of continuous change. If we take seriously that what we are is changing, developing, dynamic patterns of light, then we are connected to the entire cosmos, which is also interconnected, shifting patterns of energy. We are connected to all; there is a oneness that is bigger even than the biosphere. We are made out of the same stuff as distant galaxies and stars; there is the entire universe in us. The new science means that the problem of the body/mind dichotomy, or the spirit/body split, disappears, because mind is a name for the process that brains do in the world. Minds are not things. Minds are brains acting in a living creature in a living environment.

If that is the case, if God is the grand integration of all becoming, if God is the dynamic that makes for novelty, innovation, complexity, and growth; if God is the capacity of everything to relate to everything else, and we, therefore, partake of that godliness by our capacity to relate and innovate and create, then we are invited to rethink God's power. Dominant theologies think of God as up there/out there, while we are down here. That substance theology works through force and coercive power—God is a substance; we are a substance; there are these objects; we bang against each other externally. When substances bang against each other, one wins by the other losing. Most theologians conceive of God's power as supreme coercion—God forces things to happen or prevents them. But if we think of creation not as substances but as events, as energy patterns interrelating all the time, making choices, choosing an open future, then God's power is better conceived as persuasive. God's power is the inner unfolding of relationships, conferring the ability for us to do the right thing, "choose life" (Deuteronomy 30:19). God, at every moment, invites us to make the best possible choice given the sum total of everything that brought us to this moment. So we have all the constraints of our biology, genetics, social and cultural backgrounds, gender, lifestyle, income—all those things feed into where we are right now—plus our capacities to innovate and choose, and become something unprecedented. All of that meets us in this moment, and at this moment the future offers us infinite potential. The Divine urges the best possible choice. We know what that choice is already, not as something that descends from above but as an option that we are in contact with intuitively. "You have been told, earthling, what is good and what the Holy One requires of you" (Micah 6:8).

I do not believe in an up-there/out-there God. God is the pervasive becoming ground of all. So at this moment, we know internally what is the optimal choice. But the Divine is not coercive. This means we can disregard the divine lure. There are always alternate urges clamoring for our attention: fatigue, jealousy, ambition, hunger, loneliness, anger. It remains up to us to make our choice, intuitively recognizing God's invitation, yet also feeling the pull of our own drives and shortcomings. And then, because God is becoming, as are we, God internalizes our choice, freely made. That choice becomes objectively real in God, forever. God meets you in that new moment, offering the best choice we can make in that new instant.

The freedom of the future is ours. We are really created. God will not force our decisions, cannot force our decisions. The whole notion of *t'shuvah* is predicated, says Rambam, on freedom. In fact, the whole notion of *mitzvot* (commandments) is based on our ability to choose observance or not.

This is a very different God than the one we have been told we are supposed to believe in. It is the God you will encounter in Torah when you read it without the veneer of Greek philosophy or Newtonian physics. It is, I believe, the God you will find in the Siddur—one who cares, who relates, who invites us to make the best decisions and who remains vulnerable to our choices. And most importantly of all, if I am right, it is the God who already dwells in and through each of us. This God permeates everything that is in the process of becoming, unifying, and relating to everything that is becoming, and empowers us to live in covenant and grow in *mitzvot*, doing deeds of loving-kindness and telling stories of cosmic wisdom.

God as the Breath of Life

Eitan Fishbane, PhD

EACH YEAR AS ROSH HASHANAH and Yom Kippur draw closer—as I imagine standing in *shul*, chanting the powerful words and melody of *Avinu Malkeinu*—I am reminded of just how far I feel from that understanding of God, from the theology of "our Father, our King." For despite my connection to the language of *t'shuvah* (repentance), as well as to the inspiring music of the holiday *nusach*, I cannot affirm the literal meaning of the theology expressed on the High Holy Days, and indeed in the liturgies for daily and Shabbat prayer.

God determining and controlling all events, God sitting in judgment and doling out reward and punishment, God standing transcendent beyond this world: these are the dominant images of biblical and rabbinic theology. They permeate the canonical language of Jewish prayer. But this theology never resonated with me, never felt authentic to my spiritual quest. I could not believe in the God of heavenly transcendence, the highly anthropomorphic deity of classical Judaism. I always identified with the long history of Jewish thinkers who boldly sought to reinterpret this model. Dissatisfied with a literal understanding of scripture, many prominent theologians, from Philo of Alexandria

---

Eitan Fishbane, PhD, is assistant professor of Jewish thought at The Jewish Theological Seminary in New York. He is author of *As Light Before Dawn: The Inner World of a Medieval Kabbalist*. An earlier version of this essay appeared in the Fall 2009 issue of *CJ: Voices of Conservative/Masorti Judaism*.

onward, expressed a figurative and allegorical interpretation of that fatherly and kingly imagery, that dominant conception of determinism and omnipotence.

In our own day, the otherness of God as an enthroned king may also be reinterpreted in a decidedly non-literal way. Perhaps the kingship of God may represent the manner in which our lives are guided by the imperative and urgency of religious commandment, by the call to engage in transformative social justice. Perhaps we can adapt that image to evoke a sacred enthronement of the divine presence in nature, in ritual, in our very human hearts.

I am drawn to a theology of radical oneness, a spiritual view inspired by the mystics, one in which divinity is the totality of existence. For me, God is not beyond this world but *within* it. Divinity is the great force of life, the cosmic breath that dwells at the center of all being, the pulse of energy that runs through the cosmos, filling reality with a thousand streams of light. There, in the paths and corners of the mundane, we find the luminal presence of God. There, we are awakened to an overwhelming sense of the sacred, the Holy of Holies relocated from the ancient Temple into the human heart and the beauty of the ordinary.

The God I believe in is immanent and one with the world we know, present in the here and now, in the process of creativity, in the sublime moments of pure love, and in the very ordinary rhythms of daily life. As the *Zohar* said more than seven hundred years ago: *Leit atar panui minei*, "There is no place that is devoid of God."

And yet our experience of that fundamental oneness still allows for a sensation of transcendence, the intuition that the divine core is beyond our grasp. But instead of the heavens above, I suggest that it is the beyond within, transcendence relocated into the immanence of this world. God is the ever-present force of life in which we flourish, and yet we are perpetually mystified by that presence, ever aware that there is something profound that transcends and eludes our human perception.

We stand before the wonder of the world, and we feel the great mystery deep in our bones. The enigma of our living and our dying calls out to us. We feel the evanescence of our bodies, we search for meaning and purpose on a fragile bridge over the nothingness of unknowing.

The darkness over the face of the deep: This is our existential soul-ache, the never-ending intuition that there is more to life than we see at first glance. The mystery is as real as our senses of touch and taste; we know that there is radiance and redemption beneath the surface of our experience. That glow is the hidden light of divine presence, concealed there from time immemorial. As the ancient legend teaches, that perfect illumination was clothed in Torah. It was housed in the wondrous chambers of sacred language, in the shapes and meanings of scripture and its transmission. In each generation, the student of Torah discovers the light of those words anew, the very self of God is encountered again and again, the moment of learning an event of revelation.

The concrete markers of time and space lead us in and out of our ability to perceive this complete unity. With the entrance of Shabbat, the dining room transformed from an ordinary space into a zone of sanctity, we discover the flow of divine energy in our midst, always there, unceasing. But we cannot feel that completion in all moments; it is a spiritual state of mind and heart opened to us when we have made our souls ready, when we have attempted to live our lives with mindfulness, with attention directed to God.

The Jewish mystics teach that all of life is interconnected. We are all part of one organic whole. The wonders of nature, the transformation of the imagination before a great painting or poem, the sparkling text of Torah, the open hand of a friend—these are all pieces of the oneness of God. There is no real separation, no divide between God, the world, and our human selves. We need only look beyond the veils that cover our spiritual sight to understand the deep meaning of the biblical phrase *ein od milvado*. In its original context, this meant that there is no other God besides the God of Israel. But the Chasidic mystics read it in a boldly different way: There is nothing other than God! Divinity is all that exists. We are all but faces and traces of the great ineffable one, the pure mystery of existence that circulates through the cosmos like blood through the body.

To adapt some of the imagery used by the medieval kabbalists, God may be characterized as the ever-unfolding voice of reality, the spirit-breath that whispers and hums beneath the surface of things, slowly rising to articulation through the phenomena and happenings of this world. The nuances of the earth, the diversity of human expression and personality, the multilayered interpretations of the texts that inspire us—these are the coming-to-speech of divinity. They are the manifestations of the primordial divine word, first hidden in the mysterious chasm of cosmic memory, and then disclosed from the darkness in the present wonders of life.

If God is the great breath of the cosmos, the pulse of energy that sustains all being in every instant and every moment, then the breath of our own bodies—the force that defines our living and our dying—is the place where the divine presence is found. We live within the mystery of our mortality, of our fleeting existence in this world. All the forms that we know and love, they all return to the great ocean of oneness, to the seamless earth of the world. But from somewhere deep within, an ethereal promise of redemption shows itself, a brief vision of the ways in which we are all connected and interwoven.

And the music—the *niggun* that is God—we train our ears to hear it across the immense silence of the solitary hours: in the sound of the wind through summer's late afternoon; in the magical laughter of a child at play. The sublime sights of the eye show the word of God, the divine name that is woven into the wondrous texture of life; places that recall Eden's perfection. From ancient time, the *ru'ach* (breath; spirit) rises, slowly becoming the audible voice of reality, the evolution and distillation of the source of life. And then emerges the speech that has been there but hidden all along, the song of divinity that brings meaning to the daily rhythms of life, to the calendrical cycles of our weeks, months, and years.

In his classic of early Chasidic mysticism, *Sha'ar Hayichud v'Ha'emunah*, Rabbi Shneur Zalman of Liadi asserts that the speech of God is the very fabric of being, and were that act of speaking to stop for even a single instant, all of existence would return to *ayin v'efes mamash*, complete nothingness and nullity. This, he creatively claims, is the meaning of the verse from Psalm 119: *L'olam YHWH d'varkha nitzav ba-shamayim*, "God, Your word stands firm in the heavens forever." All of reality is animated by this eternally present divine word, the constant undercurrent of cosmic voice that maintains the life-force of all that is. Indeed, according to Rabbi Shneur Zalman, the existence of this world depends entirely upon the constancy of that divine speech, and he imagines the very texture of being as composed of the letters of supernatural utterance. The name of God itself—the tetragrammaton, YHWH—is the deep structure of reality, the life-giving speech of God that forms the shape and nature of existence. The tapestry of being is the language of God, and everywhere we look we may discover the words of divine revelation concealed in the ordinary frames of the mundane.

The history of humanity, the history of nature, these are the never-ending vibrations of God's voice. Divine revelation is the ongoing music of existence, and our souls are opened to that tone by lifting the barriers from our rigidly protected hearts to the unexpected resonance of the sacred. We become *keilim*, instruments, of the divine melody. Rising from the first breath, the life-force of God moves forward from the hidden to the revealed, from the inwardness of breath to the music of sound, the meaning of a world spoken into being. In prayer, in our moments of greatest closeness to God, we enter into the words only to move beneath them, to that region within, that place of no words. Eyes closed, the music in and through us, we feel that presence once more, the power of the chant to bring us back to a pure place of connectedness, complete integration into the oneness of all.

This is the great power of *niggunim*, the wordless contemplative melodies we chant in prayer. The *niggun* returns us to that place before language, before thought. The sounds reverberate in our souls, rousing primal memory, the perfect absorption in God that precedes all worldly form. Before the separateness of letters and words, there is pure breath and tone, song that may lead us to the moment where end meets beginning, where redemption arches back to complete the circle of creation. In *niggun* we feel the deep oneness of existence, the rhythm of a divine life-force that returns us to the pulse and drumbeat of our innermost hearts. In the domain of words and language, it is only poetry that has the power to lift us beyond the rational divisions of language and thought. Poetry, a form of music, leads us to the transcendent. Through metaphor and image, we feel the stirrings of the mysterious, we are moved to a realm where words fail us, where the mind cannot grasp and communicate the immensity of the wonder.

It is that music of Jewish devotion, the *niggun* of prayer, that may take us to the transcendent place of the speechless, the inspiration that evokes the sublime, the brilliance of the sacred. In the *niggun* we may recapture the cry of primordial yearning, the melody that guides our life-world, unseen and majestic.

Living and Dreaming with God

RABBI SHAI HELD

The Gift of *Chesed*

EVERYTHING THAT WE HAVE and are is a gift. None of us ever did any-thing—none of us *could* ever have done anything—to earn the gifts that are life and consciousness. This, I would suggest, is a key component of the spiritual awareness that Judaism seeks to instill.

Consider the following subtle but startling passage from Mai-monides' *Guide of the Perplexed* (it is difficult at first glance, but repays careful attention):

> The meaning of *chesed* is excess in whatever matter excess is practiced. In most cases, however, it is applied to excess in beneficence. Now it is known that beneficence includes two notions, one of them consisting in the exer-cise of beneficence toward one who has no right at all to claim this from you, and the other consisting in the exer-cise of beneficence toward one who deserves it, but in greater measure than he deserves it. In most cases the

Rabbi Shai Held is cofounder, Rosh HaYeshiva, and chair in Jewish thought at Mechon Hadar in New York City. He served for six years as scholar-in-residence at Kehilat Hadar and was director of education at Harvard Hillel. He is writing a book on the theology of Abraham Joshua Heschel.

> prophetic books use the word *chesed* in the sense of prac-
> ticing beneficence toward one who has no right to claim
> this from you. Therefore every benefit that comes from
> God, may God be exalted, is called *chesed*…. Hence this
> reality as a whole—I mean that God, may God be exalted,
> has brought it into being—is *chesed*. Thus it says: "The
> world is built up in *chesed*" (Psalm 89:3), the meaning of
> which is: the building-up of the world is *chesed*.[1]

Let's translate the philosophy-speak into more straightforward English: *chesed* means excess, usually excess in kindness. Excess kindness comes in two forms—either someone has no right to anything, but I nevertheless choose to give her something, or she has the right to something, but I choose to give her more than what she can rightly claim. When the prophets speak of God's *chesed*, they use *chesed* in the former sense, since, after all—and here's the core claim—God owed us nothing, and yet chose to bring the world into being and thus to give us something. The world, and our life within it, is a product of God's grace and loving-kindness.

What does all this mean? Judaism is, at bottom, a religion of grati-tude. Nothing is more antithetical to Jewish spiritual awareness than an overweening sense of entitlement, and nothing more indicative of a Jewish approach to life than an abundant sense of appreciation. Tradi-tionally, Jews begin each day with three simple words: *modeh* (or *modah*) *ani l'fanecha*, "grateful am I before You." Note that we do not say *ani modeh* ("I am grateful"), but *modeh ani* ("grateful am I"), as if to suggest that there is no self without gratitude, that I do not become fully human unless and until I convey my gratitude to the One who cre-ated the gift that I am, and the even greater gift that I inhabit.

To be spiritually awake is to ask, why is there something rather than nothing? Because, Judaism teaches, of God's grace. (To take the world for granted, to see it as a mere brute fact, is to betray a kind of spiritual deadness.) We can already see that Jewish theology and Jewish spiritual-ity go hand in hand. A theological claim—God created the world out of nothing—is inextricably woven with a spiritual perception and commit-ment—life is a wondrous gift for which we must be perpetually grateful.

What are we to do with this realization of our having been created, with our sense that we have arrived in this world not through our own efforts but through the grace and kindness of God? Put simply, we are called to give what we have been given. Having received an inestimable gift of *chesed*, we are called upon to bestow *chesed* ourselves. This is the underlying basis of Judaism's highest spiritual ideal: that we walk in God's ways by becoming compassionate and merciful.

In the Image of God[2]

Judaism does not tell us merely that we are created, but rather also that we are created *in the image of God (tzelem elohim)*, and are therefore infi-nitely valuable and beloved of God.[3] To be a serious Jew, then, is to strive to affirm the dignity and value of every person. But it is also to live with an often excruciating tension. On the one hand, Judaism tells us that every human being matters in an ultimate way. On the other hand, we live with the reality that human dignity is trodden and trampled upon in countless ways—by cruelty and callousness, by illness and disease, by deprivation and desperation, and by pervasive hunger, poverty, oppres-sion, and loneliness. The extent of human suffering threatens to reduce our belief in *tzelem elohim* to so much cant and nonsense. It is in the yawning chasm between this foundational assertion of Jewish theology, on the one hand, and our daily experience of that assertion's being not yet true, on the other, that the covenant between God and Israel is born.

By creating human beings, God has taken an enormous risk, the risk that God will be painfully and repeatedly disappointed. In an act of infinite love, God has chosen to need us. Judaism rises and falls with the insistence that God has entered into a relationship with the Jewish People in which we are called upon to help narrow the enormous gap between the ideal and the real. God's dream is of a world in which human dignity is real and the presence of God is manifest. To be a covenantal Jew is to dare to dream with God.

I want to emphasize that there are two critical and intertwined mandates here: creating a just and compassionate society; and entering into a conscious, explicit relationship with God. Too often in liberal presentations of the Jewish tradition, the latter imperative is elided or simply collapsed into the first. To be clear, a just and compassionate world is a crucial and constitutive piece of God's dream, but it alone does not exhaust it. Since evil and suffering are the biggest obstacles to human recognition of the Divine, the elimination (or, at least, the dramatic mitigation) of the former makes the latter more possible. Recall that Pharaoh is ordered not merely to "let My people go," but rather to "let My people go *that they may worship Me*" (Exodus 7:26).

If covenant is the bridge between the world as it is and the world as it must be, Halakhah is the language with which we tell God's story. It is the way in which we as a people give voice to our most treasured memories and our deepest aspirations, the path by which we attempt to introduce the sacred into the mundane, the holy into the otherwise merely profane. Most importantly, Halakhah is our attempt to instantiate prophecy, to implement and embody the ideals that Torah holds dear—the ideals of love and holiness, justice, compassion, and goodness. "*Chakham adif minavi*" (BT *Bava Batra* 12a), the Rabbis tell us, "The sage is preferable to the prophet." The reason for this is clear, Rabbi Abraham Isaac Kook insists: prophets are especially good at lamenting evil and idolatry and articulating the lofty ideals of love of God and humanity, but they are less effective when it comes to the problems of implementation, of getting the world from here to there. It is the sage who works to translate the grand ideals of prophecy into the realities of everyday life.[4] All of this is a way of saying something at once simple and profound: prophecy without Halakhah easily descends into empty platitude, while Halakhah unmoored from prophecy too often ceases to be *about* anything at all.[5]

Let me state this as clearly as I can: Halakhah is not enough. Judaism has a clear vision of the kind of human beings it wants us to become. We are required to observe *mitzvot*—no small task, to be sure—but that is only the baseline. Torah asks us not merely to obey measurable laws, but to "walk in God's ways," that is, the Rabbis explain, to clothe the naked, visit the sick, bury the dead, and comfort the bereaved.[6] We are asked to become like God by being creatures of *chesed*, love manifested as kindness. Even more profoundly, we are asked to transform our own suffering into love—to love the stranger, because, after all, we "know the feelings of the stranger."[7] To become a Jew in the deepest sense is to cultivate one's innate capacity for compassion and to strive to serve as an earthly reflection of God's own infinite compassion.[8]

Universalism vs. Particularism

I have spoken a great deal about Judaism's concern with the world and with the human beings who inhabit it. There is no way around it: at heart, Judaism has profoundly universalistic concerns. It is Adam, not Abraham, who is the first human being, and it is the earth in general, not the Land of Israel in particular, that God creates during the six days of creation. But Jewish universalism is always dialectical. Consider the words that begin God's relationship with (to be anachronistic) the Jewish People. Abram is told to leave behind everything familiar, to go his own separate way (particularism), but is then promised (challenged?) that all the families of the earth shall be blessed through him (universalism) (Genesis 12:1–3).[9] Too many Jews in the modern world have succumbed to one or the other temptation, either to care about the Jews and effectively ignore the rest of the world or to care about the whole world and forget their own identity and covenantal destiny. These temptations are no less lamentable for their being, perhaps, understandable. Recall Hillel's famous (and over-quoted) dictum: "If I am not for myself, who will be for me; but if I am only for myself, what am I?" (*Pirkei Avot* 1:14). The Jew, I would propose, is asked to live in the semicolon between the two questions. The Jew, in fact, *is* that very semicolon.

To Work and to Wait

God's presence in the world is not always obvious. At times it seems as if we inhabit a godless world, overrun by forces of barbarism and brutality. Tragically, unconscionably, religion itself (and let us not delude or flatter ourselves; Judaism, too) can often function as the most potent tool of those very forces. The Torah we teach, the Torah we embody (and let us never forget, the Torah we embody *is* ultimately the Torah we teach), must be a *Torah shel chesed*, a Torah of love and kindness. It is through lives of *chesed* that we become truly human, but also through them that God's presence is, as it were, returned to the world.

To take God's covenant seriously is to affirm, with the Exodus, that the status quo is not all there is, that another world—again, a world in which human dignity is real and the presence of God is manifest—is possible. We are called upon both to work and to wait: to work for a world that comes closer to realizing God's dreams, and to wait for God to complete the task by bringing the ultimate redemption. (Be careful of human beings who think they can accomplish that task themselves; messianic pretenders are a dangerous lot.)

There is no greater covenantal tragedy than a Jewish People that thinks that Judaism means either piety or social action. On the contrary, Judaism means piety *and* social action, love of God and love of neighbor. To embrace a life of Torah and *mitzvot* is to set one's heart aflame with the desire to know God, to serve God, and to help God find a dwelling place in this often dark and cruel world. It is this that Judaism asks of us: to love God, to do *chesed*, and to understand—heart, mind, and body—that the two are inextricably intertwined.

To be created in the image of God is to be born with a hunger for God, an inner yearning for closeness with the One who brought us into being and sustains us in life. Ideally, the life of covenant will nurture this innate but often inchoate connection, making conscious and explicit what too often remains merely unconscious and implicit. I have moved between speaking of the redemption of the whole world and of the awakening of our own individual souls. This is Torah's magic and its challenge—to perceive and embody the sacred fusion of the two.

Cosmic Theology and Earthly Religion

RABBI JEREMY KALMANOFSKY

GOD IS INFINITE and eternal. I am mortal and particular. God is not Jewish. I am. These polarities supply structural foundations to my religious life. Through them, I can affirm what true monotheists know: the cosmic God is too big to be contained in the boxes of any human culture. At the same time, when I approach ultimate transcendence, I am defined by a particular cultural identity, with a limited but profound repertoire of sacred words and deeds.

Let us begin with the big and get smaller. The cosmos is so vast it silences the mind. Let light be, said *elohim*, and the universe exploded in a Big Bang, nearly fourteen billion years ago, triggering a still-accelerating expansion of space. We earthlings detect visible light from more than fifteen billion light years away and estimate that we detect expanses of space more than ninety billion light years across. We live on a nothing-special planet, orbiting a nothing-special star, in a middling galaxy, one of hundreds within the Virgo supercluster, itself just one of millions of superclusters. One billion light years from us lies the biggest of all, the Sloan Great Wall, a row of galaxies 1.37 billion light years long. Literally, sextillions of stars!

Rabbi Jeremy Kalmanofsky serves at congregation Ansche Chesed in New York City, where he lives with his wife and four children.

Our ancestors thought heaven's grandeur indicated God's majesty (Isaiah 40, Job 38). They had no clue. We see this terrifying, obliterating truth more clearly. Is it possible that in all this vastness, a special divine drama just happens to be enacted on our planet? Starring our particular clan? Is it possible that in all that space-time we find ourselves living just a cosmic nanosecond since God revealed Torah? Living just a cosmic micrometer away from the sacred mountains of Sinai, where God descended, and Zion, where God caused the divine name to dwell? Is it possible that of all the species of life on earth, let alone in the universe, we happen to be the one fortunate enough to bear the divine image, *tzelem elohim*? How was God manifest during the 99.99999 percent of time before *homo sapiens* evolved? Where will God's image be after we evolve away?

Theologically, I must conclude that all this cannot be about us. Our narcissistic little species is inclined to view ourselves as protagonists in cosmic dramas of exile and redemption, rebellion and surrender, sin and salvation. We usually fail to absorb what Copernicus proved half a millennium ago: that we do not live at the center of the universe. We still theologize geocentrically. Contemporary Judaism needs a faith befitting a cosmos; a faith that does not narrow the infinite God to the infinitesimal conditions of our times and places. Two and a half millennia ago, biblical theology developed haltingly beyond the worship of a single, locally dwelling God who was only the biggest and nearest among many divine powers—the fancy term for this is *chthonic henotheism*—to true monotheism, the affirmation that *Adonai hu ha-elohim,* that *hashem* alone is God, in heaven above and earth below. *Ein od,* there is nothing else (Deuteronomy 4:39). Contemporary Jews should undergo a similar development, further refining our monotheism, affirming that God is no earthling.

Yet we are earthlings, born from dust, fated to return to dust. And perhaps Judaism's greatest spiritual achievement is to correlate each atom of our earthliness to cosmic significance. Through laws on how to eat and feed others, how to do business and build homes, ways of having our babies and burying our parents, our tradition affirms that our earthly lives align with the ultimate, beyond the earth; that in our bodies, we concretize the spiritual and spiritualize the concrete.

Modern Jews are generally better at religious anthropology than at theology. Given the limits of our metaphysical understanding and our often-excellent understanding of ourselves, we prefer thinking about a human religious culture, Judaism, to thinking about God. But Jewish theology must do both. Ignoring the cosmic dimension would leave us with a puny God—not really a monotheistic God at all, just the mightiest local power. But ignoring the earthly dimension would make God so remote from our lives that each would become pointless.

What Jewish resources can bolster a faith confronting God beyond while taking seriously the Jewish human within? I turn to a central theme in Kabbalah: the paradoxical tension between *Ein Sof*—literally, the infinite—and *sefirot*, God as manifest in endlessly diverse aspects of the life we know.

Before creation is *Ein Sof*, cosmic divinity, source of being. I find much meaning in the fact that our four-letter Hebrew name for God, *YHWH*, derives from the verb *to be*. Colloquially, we often refer to this name (and avoid pronouncing it explicitly) by transposing the letters and calling it *Shem Havaya*, literally, the "Name of Existence." On earth and in worlds beyond, across sextillions of stars and in subatomic spaces, God is the Name of Existence—its breathing and its beating heart. (Forgive such animalian metaphors for *Ein Sof*, but, being an animal myself, my conceptual repertoire is limited.)

Finding God inhering naturalistically in all things—a theory usually called *panentheism*—is the only adequate religious response to science. Theology that cannot face brute facts about cosmology and evolutionary biology is hopeless. But to treat existence only as a brute fact—as one hears from recent atheist writers such as Richard Dawkins—is meaningless. *Ein Sof* appears as the *sacred* character of all reality: ultimate, transcendent, pervasive, living goodness—indeed, the paradigm of goodness. The universe is not only big, and its creator not only mighty. They are loving, and a source of blessing even when we feel pain; they are orderly even when there are patches of chaos.

25

I see no religious response to the scope of space and time other than worshiping the Name of Existence—the sacred reality in which we participate, but that utterly transcends our place in the cosmos, let alone our cultural categories. As it should be. All theologians agree that any God worth the name should surpass our comprehension. Yet too often we assent verbally to this idea while actually still conceiving of God as a giant earthling. Sticking too closely to our home planet, we find ourselves worshiping not God, but a character in the Bible. With awe and trembling, I must concede that the character in the Bible is not God, after all, but a noble human rendering of our encounter with the ultimate reality.

Calling God by the Name of Existence challenges us as we try to adhere to some core Jewish doctrines. (Indeed, I find myself espousing a theology close to that which got Baruch ben Michael Spinoza excommunicated back in 1656. But that is postmodern Judaism: welcoming our heretics home.) Since the very point of this theology is to look beyond the local, we cannot imagine that only Israel knows the true Name of Existence or possesses the only covenant with God. Philosophers and mystics stand in equally profound awe before the ineffable mystery. How can Cosmic Being issue the commandments or redeem Egyptian slaves? *Ein Sof* cannot explain why bad things happen or why the wicked prosper. The Name of Existence doesn't *do* anything. It just *is*.

Conventional religion demands different theological tropes. God encountered in earthly life is smaller and more dazzling than the silence of infinity, summoning from us a different theological vocabulary: *sefirot*, diverse aspects of divine unity. In kabbalistic terms, *Ein Sof* is clear water, while *sefirot* are like colored glasses through which the water flows, changing hues as it hits life's diverse lights (cf. R. Moshe Cordovero, *Pardes Rimonim* 17d). Or take a different image: *Ein Sof* is white light, but when refracted through the prism of life, an underlying spectrum of color emerges.

Ein Sof is changeless. All rivers run to the sea; we are born and die, fight and love, heal and kill, but the universe abides forever. The ever-moving *sefirot* stand in tension with all that stasis. Macroscopically, the cosmos remains still. But through the lenses of human perception, we see the infinite unfold on earth as God, full of personality. This, at last, *is* the character in the Bible (and other religious literature), constantly changing in response to the world, showing joy and distress, affirming, condemning, sometimes severe and sometimes overwhelmingly warm, simultaneously male and female, wise, attentive, forgiving, and insistent. This is the God you can talk to, can love, and before whom you must give account. God of Abraham, God of Isaac, God of Jacob, not of the philosophers and savants.

Only such imaginative, intensely specific language can make sense of such a practical religion as Judaism, with its system of sacred social behavior. As infinite goodness unfolds fractally in this world, we hear a God capable of anger commanding us to confront evil. Finding reality bathed in love, we translate the Name of Existence into a tender God, calling us to love each other. Experiencing cosmic blessing, we encounter a generous God commanding us to share blessing by giving *tzedakah*. Gazing at the cosmos we see *logos,* meaningful order; gazing at earth, we encounter a wise God teaching us Torah, demanding that we order society justly. Feeling ourselves belonging to existence, we call *Ein Sof* "loving parent" and discover ourselves, in our mortality, bearing the divine image. That is why we hear existence affirming that we are infinitely valuable and commanding us to sanctify our bodies, our food, our shelter, our clothing.

One important idea emerging from the polarity of the cosmic and earthly is this: religion and theology are not identical. Theology is discourse about God. Religion is the human, social response to transcendence; systems of ideas, tales, and behaviors that help us keep faith with our deepest spiritual experiences. This is true of Judaism, as of Islam, Christianity, and the rest. Normative Judaism provides an excellent, time-tested path for sanctifying our minds, morals, and bodies (cf. *Guide for the Perplexed* 3:27), refining us as people, improving the world, correlating our lives to the infinite God unfolding on the finite earth.

That is why we should adhere to normative Judaism with devotion. Not because God gave it to Moses in written form. Nor because it is the only true spiritual path in this world. Certainly not because cosmic transcendence stretches only as far as a gigantic earthling whose clock runs on seven-day solar weeks and 29.53-day lunar months, and whose will is inextricably bound to such biological accidents as the bovine ruminant stomach and the twenty-eight-day human menstrual cycle. Rather, we should adhere to normative Judaism because it is our people's response to encountering the ultimate in the small. Detecting the infinite in finite life, we solidify and regularize our insight in holy words and deeds. For one example, we've learned that on earth, the mighty often trample the stranger, but that sometimes slaves are liberated; that, nonetheless, sometimes slaves prefer bondage, with all the free fish that comes with it, to the terrifying burdens of freedom. And we've experienced the very Name of Existence, cosmic paradigm of goodness, calling us to affirm freedom and reject bondage. So normative Judaism commands behaviors and authorizes teachings to help us live this truth.

At their most profound, these norms should illuminate both the variegated *sefirot* within our experience and the cosmic mystery beyond it. Many contemporary Jews—especially the more observant—are reared on a kind of religious behaviorism: light candles, lay *tefillin*, don't eat ham. Others find a social gospel easier going: give *tzedakah*; justice, justice shall you pursue. All these are crucial to Jewish life. Worshiping the Name of Existence may come less naturally. But it seems to me particularly valuable in our day, given what we know of space and time, to cultivate a theological discourse of the infinite. Through Jewish history, our deepest theologians pressed toward the dimension where, in the words of the *Zohar* (2:42b, 2:239a), there is "no image, no likeness, and no form," "no will, nor illumination, nor light." "There, all is equal," said the Chasidic master Rabbi Dov Baer of Mezritch, "life and death, sea and dry land" (*Maggid D'varav L'Yaakov* 110). Even our greatest legalist Maimonides taught that, since human theology inevitably shrinks the cosmic to fit its own scanty vocabulary, the best worship is to fall silent before the reality surpassing understanding (*Guide for the Perplexed* 1:59).

For these sages, Jewish practice illuminated ultimate theological truths. I believe the practical *mitzvot* still can cultivate cosmic awareness, as I hope the following example shows. Today's Jews say *Sh'ma Yisrael* better than our ancestors ever could. The Talmud instructs that when proclaiming that God is One, you should reflect on divine dominion "above and below and to the four sides of heaven" (BT *B'rakhot* 13b). Try this: recite *Sh'ma* locally, globally, cosmically, and cellularly. Imagine God's pervasive unifying presence in the four cardinal directions in your own locale. Imagine poor neighborhoods in one direction and comfortable neighbors beside them; think of architectural marvels to one side and natural magnificence to another. *God is One.* Do the same with a wider gaze, reflecting on the planet's natures and cultures. Ice caps and Inuits to the north; Amazonian jungles to the south, myriad plants and animals, some thriving, some endangered; *Eretz Yisrael* to the east; the Pacific Ocean to the west. *God is One.* Gaze above: *God is One* in space, on all planets surrounding all stars revolving in all galaxies. *God is One* in time: billions of years backwards toward the Big Bang, when primordial forces combined subatomic potential into elements, ultimately forming radiant stellar power plants around which gravity drew debris to become planets; and trillions of years forward, when stars will sputter out and black holes swallow space, until ... nothing. As *Adon Olam* says, *v'acharei kikhlot hakol, l'vado yimlokh nora;* "when all ends, the Awesome reigns alone." For now, though, you can relax and gaze below: *God is One* in the cells of your body, composed of the same elements formed in the foundries of the stars. You are living stardust, a mortal fragment of infinity.

Contemporary Jewish theology, it seems to me, must develop a pair of truths, stretched taut in grand paradox. We must recognize *Ein Sof*, the infinite Name of Existence, in a cosmos so vast we vanish. Anything less is not monotheism. And we must see *sefirot*, the manifold colors in which infinity unfolds on earth, and which give rise to religion's sacred words and deeds.

The ancient sage Rabbi Avin expressed a most interesting vantage point on this idea in the Land of Israel in the fourth century. For all its radiance, he said, "the orb of the sun is the unripened fruit of heavenly light"; and for all its sanctity, "Torah is the unripened fruit of heavenly wisdom" (*Genesis Rabbah* 17:5). Rabbi Avin intuited that the undeniable fullness of earthly life exists within a transcendent frame of reference we can scarcely imagine. Judaism is well suited to teach this dialectic of cosmos and earth. After all, the central idea in rabbinic Judaism is that we possess Torah in two aspects, both written and oral. I would follow medieval kabbalists in developing that theme of a double Torah to understand earthly wisdom as pointing dimly to surpassing cosmic meaning: The Written Torah, God's gift to us, is existence, the texture of being, in all its vastness. In sacred smallness, Judaism is the Oral Torah, our interpretation of God's cosmic book, our gift to God.

Non-dual Judaism

Rabbi James Jacobson-Maisels

A CERTAIN KING, relates the Baal Shem Tov (the founder of Chasidism), built himself a castle fortified with countless walls, partitions, and gates. At each gate, by command of the king, treasures and gold were distributed freely to pilgrims, increasing in bounty as the gates became more inward and closer to the king. Many such petitioners who came to see the king accepted such riches readily at the outer gates and, delighted, set off on their way. A few persistent souls, however, burning with desire to see the king himself, ignored the proffered treasure and, after many travails, came into the presence of the king himself. Once in the royal presence, each one suddenly saw, as if a veil had lifted, that all the walls and partitions presented only an illusion of separation. The walls themselves were the very substance and essence of the king.[1]

God: Nothingness, Being, and Insight

This parable contains the essence of my understanding of God and the religious path. The fundamental insight it calls on us to strive to achieve and integrate is the divinity of all we encounter, the reality that there is ultimately nothing but God. Every day in the *Aleinu* prayer we

Rabbi James Jacobson-Maisels teaches Jewish thought, mysticism, spiritual practices, and meditation at the Pardes Institute of Jewish Studies in Jerusalem. He is currently pursuing a PhD at the University of Chicago in Jewish mysticism and has taught Judaism, Jewish mysticism, and Jewish spiritual practices in a variety of settings in America and Israel.

recite "*hashem* is God, in the heavens above and on the earth below, there is no other" (Deuteronomy 4:39). "There is no other," not simply no other God but no *other* of any sort.[2] We discover that everything we experience, everything we are, every being we encounter, every speck of sand is the Divine. Yet at the same time, this affirmation of divine presence, in its very nature as an affirmation and definition, limits the unlimited and bounds the boundless. Ultimately, therefore, this claim that "There is no other" is the claim of non-duality. In a combination of Maimonidean negative theology and Chasidic panentheism[3] we realize that the fundamental insight is not the positive assertion of unity, which itself can be a kind of grasping, but the negative release of all concepts, thus non-duality. The ultimate theological insight is to see the illusory nature of the walls that we imagine separate ourselves from God, the world, and other people; to see the nothingness (*ayin*) of our sense of a separate self.

At its core then, this is not a theology of relation to a divine being but one of awareness, connection, and relation to the divine nature of our experience. As Pinchas of Koretz, an early Chasidic master, teaches, "The world thinks that one prays before the Holy One, blessed be He, but it is not thus. For prayer itself is truly [*mamash*] the essence of divinity. As it is written: He is your prayer and He is your God (Deuteronomy 10:21)" (*Midrash Pinchas* 1:52). Our natural tendency is to reify, to go beyond our experience; but what would our experience be if we could simply stay with the fullness of the moment itself? What if we could see that the Beyond is present in every here and now? What if we could pray in a way that did not reach beyond prayer to some other being, but which recognized prayer itself as the very revelation of Being?

We touch this insight—a profound sense of connection, a dropping away of the self, a deep joy, and an inner freedom at our peak moments—perhaps through dedicated spiritual practice. Perhaps we encounter it through life experiences such as moments of birth or death, fortuitous circumstances or settings such as mountain peaks or ocean storms, or moments of grace, times of favor. The language of the divinity of all being, of non-duality, is an attempt to cultivate those insights and to integrate them and their entailments into our everyday life. In these moments, the barriers we erect between ourselves and others fall away and we find God as the quiet space within, the boundless loving presence, the falling away of fear, and the delight of wonder and joy. We touch *ayin*, nothingness, the deepest level of awareness of divinity beyond all duality and definition. More importantly, we become nothingness. In the wordplay of the Chasidim, the self, the I (*ani*) becomes the boundless nothingness (*ayin*). We recognize our own divine essence and its non-separation from the divine essence of all other being. We see our illusion of self shattered on the rocks of insight and watch it dissolve into the stream of awareness.[4]

We touch *ayin* (nothingness) and then return to *yesh* (being). We recognize non-duality and then return to a world of separation and distinction. The goal is not to remain in *ayin*, but to return to *yesh* with the insight of *ayin*, to emerge from non-being into new being without the prison of the self.[5] Indeed, this is the essential understanding of the parable of the castle, which describes the illusion not as the existence of the walls (i.e., the denial of reality) but as mistakenly considering the walls as barriers rather than as presence. In truth, the walls, as Rabbi Jacob Joseph of Polonne describes them, "are His very essence, may He be blessed" they are "like a snail whose garment is part of its very self."[6] So too the illusion is not the existence of some person, but the view that that person is inherently separate from every other person and the world she lives in. The basic spiritual practice called for by this theology then is the awareness of the non-separation and divinity of the world and all its inhabitants. This engenders a natural openness, wisdom, love, mindfulness, compassion, acceptance, and equanimity.[7]

The ultimate attainment, the supreme divinity, is then beyond *yesh* or *ayin*. It is neither emptiness nor fullness, being nor nothingness, unity nor separation, presence nor absence, but the non-dual awareness beyond even these distinctions. Faith then, as Rabbi Azriel of Gerona, an early kabbalist, describes it, is precisely the subtle meeting point of these two modes of relation, of *yesh* and *ayin*.[8] Faith is living in the world of *yesh* with the consciousness of *ayin* and recognizing the undifferentiated wholeness that lies behind and integrates them both. Idolatry, heresy, as Azriel then describes it, is the rejection of this unity and the affirmation of an essential differentiation. Indeed, Rabbi Menachem Nahum of Chernobyl, an early Chasidic master, teaches that one who does not see the Divine in every aspect of creation and so fails to cleave to God in every action, no matter how material, is guilty of "cutting the shoots," that is, guilty of heresy.[9] Indeed, a long kabbalistic tradition already understands the fundamental meaning of sin as separation while the deep meaning of *mitzvah* is connection.[10] If idolatry is conventionally understood as affirming the existence of another god,[11] then this mystical perspective sees idolatry as the affirmation of any other at all.

Life: Finding God in Every Moment

Living, or attempting to live, such a theology is a transformative experience. Emerging from experiences based in concentrated awareness, this way of speaking of God encourages a constant mindfulness and presence. If every moment, every object, and every being is the Divine before us, the Divine that *is* us, then we are constantly challenged to pay attention, to be aware, to hear that still, small voice and to turn aside to see the burning bush that is not consumed. We bring a freshness and openness to our experience, ready to find God in every moment. Cherishing our present experience as an encounter with divinity, we can slowly let go of excessive rumination on the past or future, on worries, mistakes, and even opportunities, and be liberated in the present moment. We embrace the world, as the Chasidim teach, with joy and wonder and what Abraham Joshua Heschel called radical amazement.

We transform ourselves not through recrimination and guilt but through discerning awareness and by awakening to our own divine nature. In realizing the sacred nature of all being, we adopt an attitude of radical acceptance to all experience and, perhaps most importantly, to ourselves.[12] Radical acceptance does not mean approval, but rather the courageous willingness to be completely present with our current reality, for it, too, is a sacred manifestation and teaching. Radical acceptance means the willingness to fully encounter the parts of the world and parts of ourselves that we find difficult, shameful, terrifying, enraging, and repulsive. As the Maggid of Mezritch teaches, when we encounter distracting thoughts in our prayer—thoughts of pride, desire, anger, or hatred—we do not reject them, but open to them fully and reintegrate them into the divine.[13]

Such a theology is similarly the midwife of compassion, helping compassion to be born in the world. Seeing each being we encounter as a manifestation of God spontaneously gives rise to feelings of love and concern for that being. Moreover, the insight of non-duality means we recognize that there is no genuine distinction between ourselves and others. Our souls, as Rabbi Moshe Cordovero describes it, are interpenetrated. There is no I without the other and no other without my participation. For this reason, no act is isolated. With this awareness, Rabbi Cordovero explains, we will experience our fellow's suffering as if it is our own and therefore truly fulfill the commandment to love our neighbor as ourself (*Tomer Devorah*, 1:4).

On an individual level, the integration of such a theology leads to the liberation from suffering. As the Baal Shem Tov (Besht) describes it, our resistance to the difficulties of life merely multiplies our suffering, but when we respond to pain with compassion and acceptance our suffering becomes joy.[14] While pain may be inevitable, suffering—the hurt we generate by our reaction to life's circumstances—is not and non-dualism provides its release.

The joy and openness of realizing divine presence similarly removes suffering and want. It does so not through satisfying our desires but through the realization that the joy of presence can be attained even in the midst of unsatisfied desires. Fulfillment comes not from desirous satisfaction but from boundless sacred awareness, from fully opening to the world just as it is. Moreover, this expansive view places our often petty concerns in perspective, not just intellectually but experientially, in the joy of unbounded presence. As the Besht teaches in regard to prayer, when we recognize God's presence and pray from that awareness, our requests are automatically answered from that very awareness itself. That is, the Besht provides here a mystical-naturalistic understanding of providence that sees our fulfillment—the erasure of want and suffering—as rising naturally from the realization of divine presence. It is not that all our desires are answered, but that we no longer have to suffer when they are not.

All of these elements—joy, awareness, compassion, openness, freedom from suffering, and others—are rooted in the falling away of self, the movement from *ani*-I to *ayin*-nothingness. This letting go of self is the deep *p'shat* (the literal meaning) of the Jewish focus on humility as a core virtue and practice.[15] In seeing ourselves as an integrated element of God, in letting go of our illusions of essential differentiation, and in acquiring humility, that is, the abandonment of ego, these virtues naturally arise. As the Maggid of Mezritch describes it, when we see the holy everywhere, when every sense, whether sight, hearing, smell, taste, or touch, recognizes it is apprehending the Divine, then selfish desires fall away.[16] This dropping away of self, of separation, gives rise to compassion as we see our connection with others. It erases suffering and cultivates expansiveness as we no longer need to protect our ego from assault and can let our walls and armor crumble. The clinging, rejection, and separation that block the pure clarity and joyousness of our divine nature are removed and allow our true nature to rise.

In all these ways we realize the promise of being created in the divine image. Whether in Rabbi Cordovero's interpenetrated self and the parallel interpenetrated nature of the *sefirot*, in the Maggid's rooting of self in nothingness and the parallel deep nature of divinity, or simply the recognition that the claim "there is no other" includes us as well, our lack of self, non-separation, and unity with all being is merely a reflection of the non-dual nature of divinity. Indeed, the theological meaning of being in the divine image is that our claims about God are, in truth, claims about ourselves.

Torah

How then do we understand Torah and revelation on such an approach? On one level, all reality including ourselves becomes Torah, for everything is a revelation of divinity. As Torah ourselves, we must recognize how our own person reveals the divine presence, and we must study ourselves intensively, going deeper and deeper, from the surface concerns of our *p'shat* (the literal meaning) to the fathomless nature of our *sod* (the mystical meaning).[17] Introspection, mindful self-awareness, then becomes *talmud Torah* (study of Torah). By delving into the mystery of the self we uncover the divine revelation within. Yet not only ourselves, but all reality is Torah.[18] We are called upon to carefully read and study every experience, object, and moment for they are all, as Torah, revelations of God. We are asked to treat every instant with the passion and focus we aim to bring to our *talmud Torah;* every bite of food, every conversation with the sanctity of a *sefer Torah* (Torah scroll).

This expansion of Torah does not mean, however, that Torah proper loses all meaning. While at the level of *ayin* there are no distinctions, in our lives—in the realm of *yesh*—Torah, Written and Oral, still has a different status and meaning than other texts. While revelation can happen in any moment, the revelation at Sinai has a particular significance for Israel. So what then is the nature of that revelation? Was Torah given word for word to Moses in both written and oral form? The Talmud discusses to what extent revelation was heard by all Israel and to what extent it was given only to Moses, suggesting that only the first two commandments were heard by all (BT *Makkot* 24a). Rabbi Menahem Mendel of Rymanov, an early Chasidic master, develops this theme and suggests that, in fact, all that was said by God was the first letter of the first commandment, an *alef*.[19] The silent *alef* indicates that revelation on this conception takes place at the level of *ayin*, the level of silence beyond language, beyond concept, beyond differentiation.[20] Moses's genius was his ability to translate this *ayin* into *yesh*. Yet its manifestation as *yesh* can never capture its fullness. Thus we have midrashic and kabbalistic suggestions of a missing book of Torah, a repunctuation of Torah, a rearrangement of the letters, or a new Torah to emerge in the eschaton.[21] Similarly, conceptions of *machloket* (debate), which see "these and these as the words of the living God," understand that behind this multiplicity lies an undifferentiated source that unifies opposites (BT *Eiruvin* 13b).

The Torah we encounter, therefore, is always a particular instantiation of the primordial Torah that it expresses. The Torah of *ayin* is transformed into a particular *yesh* through human beings trapped in their own time, culture, and personalities, and so is not yet whole and calls on us to complete it.[22] As emerging from a deep experience of *ayin* and from the unique persona of Moses,[23] Torah has a unique status as revelation. Yet given its differentiated, partial and (time-space-person) specific nature as *yesh*, and given its redacted nature from different traditions, Torah can be mistaken at the *peshat* level. Our task is to discover the truth emerging from the experience of *ayin* when we delve to the level of *sod*.

Mitzvot: Mindfulness Training

Mitzvot provide a system of spiritual practices that aim to lead us to the realization of divine presence. The *Sefat Emet*, in one context, deems *mitzvot* as "advice" on how to attain liberation.[24] The Chasidic text *Mei Hashiloach* similarly understands *mitzvot* as practices of self-clarification that ultimately bring us to the awareness of the omnipresence of divinity.[25] In this sense, as the Maggid of Mezritch teaches, there are not only 613 *mitzvot* but infinite *mitzvot,* as every action can fulfill the commandment to "know Him in all your ways" (Proverbs 3:6).[26]

Mitzvot are then training in mindfulness, a series of practices to bring us to the awareness of the divinity of all experience. They are, as Maimonides describes them, a practice of constant focus on the Divine,[27] or, as the Rabbis explain, a means of creating connection, of recognizing the non-separation of ourselves from the All.[28] In some cases, such as the saying of blessings before a meal or the giving of *tzedakah*, the mindful, compassionate, and non-dualistic aspects of the practice are clear. In other cases, restrictions are introduced, such as *kashrut*, to train us in non-attachment and the letting go of the many elements from which we build our sense of self.[29] At times, the goals of certain *mitzvot* are not clear, yet I practice them from the trust that there is wisdom in the system even if I have not yet discovered it in this particular instance. Indeed, part of the way *mitzvot* function as a spiritual practice is their commandedness, the fact that a person is not free to choose whether to keep Shabbat this week but is compelled to do so, cultivating two crucial spiritual dispositions: humility and submission.[30]

Yet so often Halakhah seems concerned with separation rather than unity. The very meaning of holiness is rooted in the idea of being separate and set apart. We should not, however, mistake the path for the goal. Notions of separation, purity, retreat, and cessation are crucial to our development and maintenance of a consciousness of divinity. All may be divine, but the cessation of Shabbat gives us an opportunity to cultivate that awareness in a way that is difficult in the hustle and bustle of the workday week. Similarly, as the Maggid of Mezritch teaches, every act *can* be a *mitzvah*, a deep spiritual practice, yet we still need particular practices that *demand* our attention and so call on us to focus, reconnect, and awaken once more. Perhaps the perfected individual, as the *Mei Hashiloach* suggests, would no longer need *mitzvot*, but as long as we have not reached perfection they remain a crucial practice.[31]

The ultimately goal-directed nature of *mitzvot* is, however, relevant to their practice and formation. *Mitzvot*, as with any ritual, can be done automatically and thoughtlessly, devolving into what Abraham Joshua Heschel terms religious behaviorism. For *mitzvot* to fulfill their purpose, we must therefore bring mindfulness and intention to their practice. In addition, some *mitzvot*, or some aspects of them, may no longer—or may have never—fulfilled that purpose, either because of changing social circumstances or because of the imperfect *yesh*-filtered nature of the human perception of the divine *ayin*. Understanding the deep goal of *mitzvot* gives us a ground from which to transform and evolve Halakhah as necessary, to understand the underlying purpose of each *mitzvah* and ensure that its practice continues to meet that purpose.

Tikkun Olam and *Tikkun* of the Self

"I turn my eyes to the mountains, from where [*ayin*] my aid will come?" (Psalm 121:1). In moments of suffering, doubt, fear, and confusion, we lift our eyes to God hoping for salvation. In the noble dignity, the quiet strength, and the majestic spaciousness of the mountain, we find our answer. Our salvation comes not from some being, but in our awareness of *ayin*.

Recognizing the divine presence, relinquishing our illusion of separation, we acquire the dignity, strength, and spaciousness to meet suffering and confusion with compassion and presence. We, as manifestations of divinity, bring healing to ourselves, our communities, and the world in our awakening to our own sanctity and the sanctity of all others. Our task is to awaken to our boundless divine nature, to see through the walls and ramparts that keep us from the Divine and from each other, and so to restore the primordial unity and bring healing to the world.

THE GODS OF
THE TEXT

Open-Source Covenant

RABBI JONATHAN CRANE, PhD

IT IS NOT EASY TO THINK about a relationship with God. Some people skirt this issue by denying God's existence altogether. For them, it is a closed topic: there cannot be any such relationship because the other party is not there. Humankind exists only alongside the other sentient and living entities on earth; there is nothing beyond. Our relations, the deniers claim, are here with the living and not with the supposedly living.

It is plausible to be Jewish and retain a denier's position: no God, no relationship. This position is not the norm, however, in either Jewish history or the Judaic textual tradition. Rather, ever since the earliest days of Jewish existence, Jews have struggled with the idea of a relationship with God, and Jewish texts overflow with testaments to this ongoing struggle. The Hebrew term for this relationship is *b'rit*. Translating *b'rit* as a contract as do some scholars only confuses things, for the relationship between God and humankind—if there is one—cannot be a contract as we understand contracts today. It cannot be a relationship between relatively equal parties, with starting and ending dates, punishments for breaches, rewards for compliance, and causes for termination. Moreover, a contract becomes a contract precisely at that moment when both parties voluntarily agree to its details. A *b'rit* is something

Rabbi Jonathan Crane, PhD, a former Wexner Graduate Fellow at Hebrew Union College–Jewish Institute of Religion, is a visiting instructor at the University of Toronto. His scholarship focuses on contemporary Jewish thought, law, and ethics.

radically different than a contract if for no other reason than the parties thereto are not relatively equal to each other. Also, consent is not always a necessary condition for *b'rit*. For this reason, it is better to translate *b'rit* as covenant.

So what is covenant? Who declares a covenant into existence? How are the relationship's duties determined? What freedom does a covenant extend to its participants? Such inquiries into authority, reason, and autonomy have long fascinated Jews, and I am no exception. My own theology, maturing as it is, emerges from encountering the diverse and ongoing deliberations about what *b'rit* means. The following offers a brief survey of some of the more famous notions of covenant mentioned in the Jewish textual canon. I conclude with some thoughts about these sources.

Of the many covenants mentioned in the *Tanakh*, four stand out as particularly interesting. The first covenant is that between God and Noah (Genesis 6:18–20; 9:8–17) in which God promises not to destroy life again and for which the rainbow serves as a perennial reminder of this promise. Two things are noteworthy in this *b'rit*. First, God voluntarily relinquishes the right to act arbitrarily, a right God apparently exercised prior to declaring this relationship a covenant. And second, God's promise to remember to respect the living reflects an assumption that upholding promises itself is a necessary component for an intelligible and just universe.

The second, and most famous biblical covenant, is the one announced at Mount Sinai (Exodus 19–24). Here God, through Moses, makes an offer to the People Israel:

> "Now then, if you will obey Me faithfully and keep My covenant, you shall be My treasured possession among all the peoples. Indeed, all the earth is Mine, but you shall be to Me a kingdom of priests and a holy nation." (Exodus 19:5–6)

While God makes this offer via Moses and not to the people directly, the people are just far enough away to witness that God speaks to Moses but too distant to decipher what precisely God says. The people respond to God's offer individually but univocally, "All that God has spoken we will do" (Exodus 19:8). God later enumerates the content of the covenant, known as the *Aseret HaDibrot* (the Ten Words) (Exodus 20), which Moses declares as "all" that God speaks (Exodus 24:4).

What does this "all" mean? The notion of "all" or completeness is intelligible only in a conceptual universe in which lack and excess are possible. The idea that "all" has been communicated assumes that it is possible to communicate less than the full amount. Conversely, "all" also assumes that there is more that enables assessing whether everything has indeed been included in the "all." What, then, does Moses mean when he says God has spoken "all" the entailments of the *b'rit*? If it means that the totality of the covenant's stipulations is expressed here, it radically undermines the authority of later Judaic normative texts such as Halakhah. If, on the other hand, "all" here allows for later normative texts to have authoritative claim upon Jews, then Moses begs the question: what does "all" mean if it does not mean "all"? This tension is critical to the contemporary debate about whether moral guidance exists beyond Halakhah and if it should guide Jewish behavior. Either way, the ancient audience, made up of individuals acting in concert, accedes to God's offer, a gesture of acceptance not found in the Noahide covenant.

The third covenantal moment comprises two expressions when Moses recapitulates the covenant at Horeb and then at Moab. The Horeb covenant is famous for its insistence that God establishes a covenant "with us, the living, every one of us who is here today" (Deuteronomy 5:3), and its content is the slightly adjusted *Aseret HaDibrot*. The Moab covenant, by contrast, includes a lengthy enumeration of laws and rules (Deuteronomy 6–29). Only at their end does Moses gather together the people and declare that this is a covenant with God, though this one needs and complements the one articulated at Horeb. In this way the covenants Moses expressed at Horeb and Moab displace God as the sole authority who declares covenants into existence, enumerates their content, and gathers the intended parties to it.

The prophet Jeremiah offers a dramatically different notion of covenant when he speaks of a new covenant (*b'rit chadashah*). For him, a new covenant would be forged in the seat of human intellection and would not require words or commands (Jeremiah 31:33–34). People endowed with such divine wisdom would then either intuit or know outright what the covenant demands of them. Put differently, when humans think, their thoughts would be Torah, the will of God.

The Rabbis of old take inspiration from these diverse biblical covenantal ideas and construct their own theories. Some talmudic sages, for example, imagine God holding Mount Sinai over the heads of the Israelites and saying to them: "If you accept the Torah, well and good. But if you do not, there will be your grave" (BT *Shabbat* 88a). Some scholars find this vision of divine coercion repugnant, for it belittles the theological audience. On the other hand, the talmudic sages go on to interpret this vision to mean that the Israelites have the existential freedom to reject the covenant; they have the legal right to annul it; and they have the historical wherewithal to grant or withhold from it retroactive authority. An early midrash, by contrast, depicts God as a king who asks the people to accept his rule and they retort, "What good have you given us?" In response, the king performs the needful for the people, after which they accede to his request to reign over them (*M'khilta D'rabbi Yishmael, Yitro* 5). Other midrashim portray God as a peddler offering Torah to the nations of the world. These texts claim that revelation itself was promulgated in all the languages of the world so that every community could receive it, if they would. Fortunately or not, all the nations rejected Torah except Israel (e.g., *Exodus Rabbah* 5:9; *Yalkut Shimoni*, Job 921; *Sifrei Deuteronomy* 343). These and other rabbinic covenantal theories further turn attention away from God and toward the covenantal audience. The people's relative ability, freedom, and will to accept the covenant's content apparently concern the Rabbis more than the absolute authority of God. For if people have no choice whatsoever to relate with God, what would be the theological foundation for the relationship?

Medieval, early modern, and modern Jewish scholars continue wrestling with such issues as authority, reason, and autonomy. Judah

Loew ben Bezalel (Maharal) interprets the image of the overhanging mountain to mean that "Torah was voluntary on the part of Israel but necessary on God's part" (*Tiferet Yisrael* 32). The existential threat was necessary so that one cannot think that Israel's acceptance of Torah was based solely on human will, for if it was accepted by human will alone, then Torah's existence would be contingent. Baruch Spinoza, by contrast, describes the relationship between God and Israel as a contract (*pactio* or *contractum*) in which human reason abrogates to itself the authority to establish the human-divine relationship and catalog its duties. Not only is human reason the authority that declares the covenantal relationship into existence for Hermann Cohen, human reason also generates the moral ideals that serve as this relationship's content. Cohen's student, Franz Rosenzweig, however, understands the covenant to be nothing more than revelation revealing itself. Because God is no mere law giver, the covenant entails no laws, and if it has any commands, it would be the singular "Love me!" Rosenzweig argues that the covenant survives in and through human speech, for when we speak to each other we reveal the always present singular command. Martin Buber's covenantal theory defines it as a kind of self-constriction in which the participants limit themselves vis-à-vis each other and adjust the relationship's requirements to meet every historical moment's demands. Emmanuel Levinas takes Buber's relationalism further by saying that the sociality of humankind itself generates the covenantal relationship. For it is through bumping into each other that we experience the revelation that mutual yet asymmetric responsibility individuates and sanctifies us.

These theories do more than extricate God as the sole authority and primary focus of the covenantal relationship. They relocate religion, revelation, and covenant itself, not in sacrality but in sociality. They depict the moral content of this relationship as either ineluctably internalized or an unavoidable imperative. Whereas covenant in earlier theories was granted to the community, more recent theories see the individual as the rightful participant in the covenantal relationship.

This brief survey of covenantal theories demonstrates that consensus never existed in Jewish history about covenant. This fact suggests that the idea of a covenantal relationship with God is not a closed topic or text. Put differently, covenant remains an open source in the Judaic textual tradition. This can be understood in different ways.

The textual tradition resists offering a monolithic conceptualization of covenant. The sources' myriad and divergent theories open dramatically different doorways for us to appreciate the idea of a special relationship between Jews, individually and/or collectively, and God. These different doorways nevertheless share the assumption that there is a special relationship. Beyond this, however, each entry opens onto a unique way of conceptualizing how authority, reason, and autonomy (should) play out in Jewish lives. The diversity of possibilities precludes any argument that there is only one (right) way to understand covenant and only one method to fulfill covenantal duties. Covenant, Jewishly understood, is broad and open enough to countenance a wide array of interpretations and practices.

That classic sources do not close the book on covenant and declare the topic decided once and for all suggests that the conversation remains open. Indeed, it is open-armed and open-ended. Especially as access to Jewish texts is increasingly democratized through diverse education programs and more sophisticated electronic transmission, it is as if the textual tradition extends open arms to us to engage with it and study its depth and breadth. This invitation is not merely to gaze upon the wisdom found within its vast library. Rather, this invitation is a request—no, a requirement—for us to contribute to the centuries-old and ongoing deliberation about all things concerning Jews and Judaism. This includes the debate over the notion of covenant. Similar to open-source software, theories of covenant will only be as vital and as relevant as contemporary Jews make them. It is incumbent upon us to critique, tweak, and improve the wonderful theories bequeathed to us. Our tradition all but commands us to add our covenantal thoughts to the fray. For without our contributions, such theories risk losing their compelling qualities and our practice of them.

Though I consider covenant to be an open source, I do not conceive it to be relegated to debate in just any public domain. Covenant remains a central component of Judaism, and it is Jews who long have developed, and should continue to shape, its conceptual and practical dimensions. Even though Jews should take the lead in this conversation, no need exists to hide this debate altogether from the broader world. As history attests, secrecy about Jews' special relationship with God can lead to bloody misunderstandings. So as to prevent such misunderstandings, current covenantal theorists may find it beneficial to take the broader world into consideration when they formulate and communicate their ideas. Indeed, that many traditional theories of covenant speak explicitly of gentiles may offer inspiration toward this effort. Here again, covenantal theorizing appears like open-source software insofar as it endeavors not to discriminate against persons or groups.

Comparing covenantal deliberation and open-source (software) development is not meant to insult either *b'rit* or the contributors. Rather, this comparison suggests that the democraticization of access to Judaic texts and practices can only benefit our collective and individual theological reflections and convictions. The more who engage the textual tradition and the more who contribute to its open-armed and open-ended debates only promise to enhance the nuance and relevance of contemporary Jewish theology. This invitation extends even to those who may doubt God's existence and the meaningfulness of a human-divine relationship. It may well be that through engaging sincerely with the inviting and diverse textual tradition, deniers may come to realize that the tradition is more complex than they thought and that there is plenty of room within its corridors even and especially for those who, like me, are still figuring out which of the many open doorways to take.

More *Theos*, Less *Ology*

RABBI JEREMY GORDON

AS A JUNIOR RABBINICAL STUDENT with a passion for philosophy, I decided to tackle a modern Christian academic, systematic theology. It seemed a sensible thing to do if I planned to study for a masters in theology. I lasted fifty pages. It was a mind-numbingly dull book, stuffed with logical proofs, determined to avoid any whiff of contradiction, and set on tidying up the whole messy business of God. It was a Christian work, but it wasn't so much the Jesus-ness of the work that got to me, as the notion of a systematic relationship with the Divine. It left me cold and I ended up studying for a masters in midrash.

I prefer literary raids on the Divine to systematic logical posits; I'm very concerned with my *theos* and concerned only peripherally with *ology*. I like my theology full of color and contradiction, anthropomorphism and emotion. Attempts to construct watertight philosophical arguments about the nature of God and my Jewish relationship to the Divine feel unsuited to the messy, uneven world in which I find myself. If my theology is specific to "our time," it is to the extent that I don't necessarily share the same concerns of the philosophically minded theologians of previous generations. Unlike Louis Jacobs, the founding rabbi of the synagogue I now serve, I am not that interested in articulating a theology that the Orthodox Jewish world considers acceptable. Unlike Franz Rosenzweig, the early twentieth-century German theolo-

Jeremy Gordon is rabbi of New London Synagogue, England. He blogs at www.rabbionanarrowbridge.blogspot.com.

gian, I'm not that interested in a theology that passes muster according to the standards of Western universities. Unlike Maimonides, the pre-eminent medieval Jewish philosopher, I am not that interested in dog-matic assertions that allow me to test who is and who is not a proper Jewish theologian. None of these theological endeavours seems to help me be better: a better husband, father, or rabbi. They don't even seem to help me understand the world with more accuracy or insight.

∽

If my theology has a foundation, it is the verse "And God created the human in God's image, male and female God created them" (Genesis 1:27). To me, this verse is more than the foundation of conceptions of human rights, democracy, and the equality of all people (though that would be enough). It is also the key to the map that allows me to find a path toward heaven. The problem is this: I am finite and limited. There is so much I will never understand. I believe in infinity as a place where contradictions cease and everything makes sense—I call that place (lit-erally, *hamakom*) God, but I can't directly engage with that infinity. The direct engagement with infinity is impossible mathematically, philo-sophically, and emotionally, so I need a path. All religious people avail themselves of techniques that illuminate a path toward divinity. Temple Jews tried sacrifices; Abulafia tried mystical combination of letters. I use the images and tales passed down in the Jewish tradition I inherit, claim, and love. The Bible and rabbinic texts from the ancient period are full of images of a God expressed in human terms—outstretched arms, flaring nostrils, remembering and forgetting. I don't think the Rabbis believed in a literal Zeus-like caricature any more than Michelangelo (painter of the Sistine Chapel ceiling) believed God has a white beard and a pointy finger. It is just that these images allow us to negotiate the path toward that which is beyond comprehension in ways our human hearts and human minds can grasp. The verse suggesting the creation of humans in the image of God teaches me something about the nature of humanity, but it teaches me more about the nature of God. More precisely, it teaches me more about the way in which I have to think about God if I am to find any way of bridging the chasm between human and heavenly realms.

But I am not sure my theology arises from a single foundation, no matter how powerful a verse like Genesis 1:27 might be. My theology arises in the space between circumstance and *sefer* (book), between experience and giving myself and my faith time to respond. The process also works in reverse. Study produces the raw material that enters my mythical theologizer; life happens somewhere in the middle; and at the other end appears, on a good day, a coherent reflection on the space that exists between God and human (me).

An Example: From Circumstance to *Sefer*

I am a father of a three-and-a-half-year-old boy who recently followed a cat he had been playing with from the pavement into the middle of the road where he was struck (thankfully only a glancing non-serious blow) by a passing car. My wife and I have spent a lot of time talking about road safety with our son, and we were standing five meters away at the time, but he hadn't learned well enough and we hadn't managed to stop him. And then it struck me, God had the same problem in the Garden of Eden, and in the desert, and once the Israelites crossed into the Promised Land—God wants children who make independent decisions, but God also wants them (us) to behave precisely as God wishes. Our failure to prevent our son from breaking his leg was God's failure to prevent Adam and Eve from eating the fruit. It is the failure of wanting our dearest creations to have life and meaning and we've always been failing this way: God, you, and me.

An Example: From *Sefer* to Circumstance (*Genesis Rabbah* 30:10)

The Bible says that Noah walked with God, and it says that Abraham walked before God. The Rabbis suggest God had to support a stumbling and fallible Noah, but that Abraham was called forth from Mesopotamia to illuminate the path before a stumbling God, a deity staggering in the darkness like King Lear's blinded Lord Gloucester on his way to Dover. The talmudic master Reish Lakish suggests an analogy of a prince who needs his elders to lead the way before him. God needs us. Abraham Joshua Heschel had the perfect title for his major theological work, *God in Search of Man*. Needed as I am, as I believe we all are, I feel I have a role. I am called to action, and I should be doing what I can to light the way.

When my teachers (Neil Gillman, Paul Tillich, James Fowler) have written of brokenness in the context of theology, they have meant the brokenness of a believer's beliefs about God: childish literalisms broken into myths. But that has never been my experience. I never thought God, literally, had a white beard. I never felt the loss of that kind of innocence. The brokenness of my theology haunts God, not my faith journey. The brokenness of my theology is the brokenness articulated by the sixteenth-century kabbalist Isaac Luria. Luria told of a cosmology in which God began by creating a hollow void in the suffusing light of God's goodness—this is the origin of chaos and disorder. Then God tried to trickle goodness into this empty space but failed, like an electrician who fails to use wire of sufficient thickness to cope with a mighty power surge. The lower vessels shattered, and in the mess of order, chaos, good, and evil that resulted from the explosion we find ourselves, and our God, all trying to get along as well as we can.

I've had more insight, more comfort, and better instruction (*torah*) reflecting on biblical and rabbinic narratives of Divine-human encounters than in the hundreds of pages of discourse on the nature of etiology, determinism, and the rest of the classic subjects of academic theology I encountered before I gave up on systematic theology.

⸎

There are perhaps two problems with building a theology from texts like these, narratives about a broken and/or human-like deity who needs human support to realize God's lofty potential. First, we don't live in a world that appreciates the way narratives serve as carriers of profound truths. We live in a world that prefers its truths wrapped in philosophy, couched in the language of the academy and buttressed by logic. We consider stories to be playthings for children, but these texts are not childish; they are brave, bold, self-aware, and profoundly adult. They communicate more in image than logical positivism ever could.

Second, these kinds of texts feel dangerous, blasphemous almost, especially post-Rambam's decrying of anthropomorphism. Whenever I share texts like this in educational settings, I get challenged by those who insist on a Jewish theology in which God is a philosophical entity, too aloof for the corporeal sensibilities of midrash. (It is not that my challengers necessarily sign up to this aloof version of God, but this is, nonetheless, the kind of God they demand I offer for them not to believe in.) But I have sources on my side: verses, *sugyot* (talmudic passages), and midrashim. There are texts like this throughout our tradition, and they must be considered authentic by dint of their canonization in the classic collections of our faith.

These texts become the bulwark of my faith when I struggle to find a relationship with God. When the sun is shining and the birds are singing, I can find divinity everywhere. But when life seems nasty, brutish, and short, I turn to these texts and they give me insight and strength. The bad stuff—cancer, Alzheimer's, and much worse—breaks any attempt to construct an image of a wholly powerful and beneficent God. But the bad stuff doesn't force me outside my religious tradition. I don't feel the need to reformulate or reconstruct a new Jewish relationship with the Divine, unknown in history. Instead I excavate and dust down canonized images of God that speak to me in my brokenness. From this exercise in literary archaeology God emerges as a companion for my suffering (*ach l'tzarah*; BT *Sanhedrin* 46a), and that helps.

I am sometimes asked, usually by those who disavow a faith in God, if I ever have crises of faith. I find it an impossible question to answer in the terms of my questioners. I don't have crises of faith because my theology is built off existential crisis. It is a theology immune to being shattered by the slings and arrows of outrageous fortune precisely because it comes pre-shattered. I live in peace with my broken theology.

It could be that with all this emotion and my wish to find meaning, I am kidding myself. It could be that God is really no more than a fig leaf strategically placed over an existential vacuum. Or it could be that God really is all-perfect and perfectly unknowable. But, despite my disavowing of much of the scientific aspects of theology, I believe in testing my theological hypotheses. I test my theology in hospices and at Holocaust memorials. I test it in the context of my rabbinic workload of "hatch, match, and dispatch." I test my theology as I open prayer books and study books, when I sit in my home and when I go out on the street. The more I test, the more I feel that this exercise in textual archaeology in search of a broken deity who is in search of man—me—is true, and the more I test the more I feel existential nihilism and aloof perfection are equally false.

I claim and treasure the authenticity of articulating my theology in the language of the biblical and rabbinic tradition. It is not that I have a fear of being excommunicated—every decent rabbi should be excommunicated at some point—but rather that I want to be held by my *masorah* (tradition)—its people, its history, its wandering and wondering—especially when I am struggling to find a response to pain and suffering. I can't practice my theology in a cave or in an ivory tower. My theology belongs in a community, in dialogue with my congregants and my teachers and their teachers and their teachers' teachers going back to Sinai.

In the opening of this reflection I cast doubt on whether my theology really is specific to "our time." It is not supposed to be. It is supposed to be a theology for today in which the echoes and resonances of the tradition can be heard as fresh and powerful voices, able to help us live better when facing the challenges and opportunities of the current age.

This contribution is offered in memory of Prof. Yochanan Muffs of blessed memory, whose spirit pervades it.

A Progressive Reform Judaism

RABBI EVAN MOFFIC

MY LATE MENTOR and teacher Arnold Jacob Wolf argued that "there is no Judaism but Orthodoxy and all Jews are Reform." For Rabbi Wolf, and for me, Judaism cannot be understood outside of a system of commandments, *mitzvot*, given by God. Yet neither can it be understood without recognizing that the nature of those *mitzvot* change over time and that we have a choice as to the way we follow them. There is no Judaism without *mitzvot*, and there is no Judaism without autonomy. *Mitzvot* are what create the boundaries that define our community. The boundaries, however, are different for every synagogue, community, and individual. This core tension may seem to lead to anarchy and confusion, but it is a tension that has stood at the heart of Jewish life since the onset of modernity and is consistent with building communities of study, worship, and action. The tension is resolved only when we, as Franz Rosenzweig put it, "enter into life."

Let us examine that tension by first exploring the meaning of *mitzvah*. It is traditionally translated as "commandment." Yet, as Rabbi

Rabbi Evan Moffic is senior rabbi of Congregation Solel in Highland Park, Illinois. He was ordained at Hebrew Union College–Jewish Institute of Religion, and graduated from Stanford University. In addition to Jewish thought, he has written on American Jewish history, on Zionism, and responsa related to conversion.

Lawrence Kushner, a modern authority on Jewish spiritual life, has suggested, perhaps a better translation is "response." In performing a *mitzvah*, the *m'tzuveh*, the one commanded to perform a *mitzvah*, responds to the *m'tzaveh*, the commander. As thinking human beings, we do not respond automatically. To perform a *mitzvah* is not a reflexive action. We need to feel ourselves being commanded, summoned, called forth. Thus, we need a coherent view of the divine commander. What Rabbi Wolf is saying when he says that "all Jews are Reform" is that we choose to adopt a certain view and then respond accordingly. By making a choice, by performing *mitzvot* without coercion, we are, in effect, acting as autonomous Reform Jews.

What differentiates our movements, then, is their choice of how to understand God and what the right human response to God is. For Orthodoxy and Conservatism, for the most part, God is a divine commander. God gives us laws to follow, as developed into Halakhah and interpreted by rabbinic sages, and it is our obligation to follow them. For me, God is the partner in the covenant with Israel established in the Torah and explicated through Torah. We discover what God demands of us by studying Torah and by living within communities dedicated to living by its teachings. That is what it means to be part of the covenant. We do not discover God's will by hearing a voice from on high or by memorizing a book of laws. Each of us learns it by studying and living. We discover what God demands of us only by studying the texts that reflect our people's ongoing encounter with God.

Yet, the text itself is not the final authority in determining those demands. We also explore them through our relationships, through our life experiences, the communities we join, and other ideological prisms, such as feminism or rationalism, that shape our worldview. Torah, in other words, is always in dialogue with our lives. In fact, we can even call that dialogue "Torah." Each individual is the final authority in determining what those demands are. As Martin Buber put it, "I must distinguish in my innermost being what is commanded me and what is not commanded me." Yet, we are authentically Jewish individuals only insofar as we struggle with the various claims on our lives. A partner in a marriage is the final authority in determining whether or not to violate the trust of a spouse. Yet that choice would only be an authentically Jewish one if that partner weighed the demands of Jewish tradition and law, life circumstances, and the community in which he or she lives in making that choice.

In encountering the demands of Jewish tradition and law and arriving at a coherent theology, I give primacy to the ethical over the ritual. In other words, I see the ethical as deriving from a more truthful encounter with God, whereas the ritual laws reflect cultural norms developed over Jewish history. This controversial view—scathingly condemned by Rabbi Wolf as the original sin of Reform Judaism—predominated in early Reform Judaism, whose leaders saw the ethical teachings of Torah as the kernel of Judaism, and ritual laws as its husk. The kernel was eternal, and the husk was dispensable. My view differs only in that I see ritual laws and practices as doing more than just serving as a temporary protective cover for the ethical kernel. Ritual can enhance our ethical awareness and help preserve community by creating shared practices. Yet, the Levitical author who wrote, "Love your neighbor as yourself" (Leviticus 19:18), had, to my mind, a more accurate perception of God's will than the one who forbade mixing wool and linen in clothing.

Even the ethical demands develop over time, though, and depend on circumstances. What is seen as a reflection of God's will in one generation may not be so in another. We need only think of the Bible's acceptance of slavery to understand this truth. I also think the Rabbis recognized this pattern of change. That is why I think they highlighted the dual self-descriptions of *Torat Adonai* (Torah of God) and *Torat Moshe* (Torah of Moses). I see *Torat Adonai* referring to Halakhah, to Jewish ethical and rituals laws and practices like those, for example, of Shabbat and of mourning that have been formulated over time and passed on to us. *Torat Moshe* is our individual and communal response to those traditions. It is the way we make use of them, live by them, pass them on to the next generation. The two are not in equal balance. *Torat Moshe* is the way respond to *Torat Adonai* and is therefore primary for us. Yet, for the next generation, our *Torat Moshe* becomes part of their *Torat Adonai*. Thus, what is authentically Jewish evolves and changes.

When we recognize that what is authentically Jewish changes from one generation to another, we also confront the question of limits. We face an acute danger in doing so. Dr. Michael A. Meyer, professor of Jewish history at Hebrew Union College–Jewish Institute of Religion, points out that authenticity can be used as a sledgehammer to delegitimate any theology that does not fit one's own. Thus, the limits I propose are limits that operate for me in this generation, and they are subject to change over time. The first limit is that Judaism cannot become pure humanism. God, Adonai, cannot be excluded from our liturgy or theology. We can have different conceptions of God, as Torah itself does, but we cannot exclude God. Second, an authentic Jewish individual or community must identify with *klal Yisrael*, with the larger Jewish People. They must feel their fate and destiny as intertwined with that of other Jews. Identification does not imply agreement. Yet, Jews for Jesus, who identify with and predominatly affiliate with evangelical Christian organizations, are not authentically Jewish for this reason. Third, authentic Jewish choices must emerge out of study and struggle with Torah, with text. One of the central teachings of the rabbinic sages who reshaped Judaism after the destruction of the Temple in 70 C.E. was that the era of direct prophecy was over. God no longer speaks through individuals. God's voice can only be heard through study of Torah. Thus, to hear *Torat Adonai*, we must study. Fourth, authentic Judaism rejects a univocal approach to Torah. The rabbinic sages taught that the Torah has seventy faces. Thus, to say that one face is "the face," that one interpretative approach is the authentic approach, falls outside of the boundaries of Jewish self-understanding.

Just as Jewish tradition admits a pluralism of interpretative approaches, so it embraces a pluralistic approach to other religions. One of the lessons of modernity for every faith community is that no one religion has a monopoly on truth. As Rabbi Jonathan Sacks, the

Orthodox Chief Rabbi of Great Britain, put it, "God has spoken to mankind in many languages: through Judaism to Jews, Christianity to Christians, Islam to Muslims ... no one creed has a monopoly on spiritual truth; no one civilization encompasses all the spiritual, ethical, and artistic expressions of mankind."[1] This embrace of pluralism distinguishes Jewish teachings from those of classical Christianity and Islam. Whereas Christianity and Islam taught one God and one path to that God, the rabbinic sages believed in one God but saw multiple legitimate ways of responding to that God. Perhaps exemplifying this ideal—this faith in the dignity and truth of religious difference—is what Jews were chosen by God to do. In a world with over two thousand different religions, few tasks are more important.

An embrace of pluralism, however, does not connote acceptance of syncretism. Pluralism acknowledges the truths of other faiths, whereas syncretism seeks to meld different faiths into an incoherent whole. This issue frequently emerges in discussions of the role of the non-Jew in Jewish ritual. The *Tanakh* conveys a murky picture of the role of the *ger*, the stranger, in Temple ritual. On the one hand, the stranger is allowed to participate. On the other hand, this person is still a stranger and not a formal member of the Jewish People. The closest analogy I think we in the American Jewish community can draw from is the status of a green card holder. A person with a green card living in America has virtually all the privileges of naturalized citizens except that of voting. I see a Jewish green card holder as a non-Jewish person who is connected to a Jewish family, perhaps a spouse of a Jew raising Jewish children or a grandparent of a Jewish child. Such a person has all the privileges and responsibilities of Jewish life. He or she can read the prayers, say blessings, read from Torah, be expected to engage in acts of *tikkun olam*, and so forth. What he or she cannot do is become a bar or bat mitzvah, serve as a witness on a *beit din*, and other formal issues related to Jewish status unless he or she undertakes the process of conversion. Those who would not permit a "Jewish green card holder" to read from Torah or say certain blessings often claim that it is preposterous for someone who is not Jewish to say, for example, the blessing before reading Torah that thanks God for "choosing us from among all the peoples." This reasoning strikes me as overly literalist. Just as we interpret blessings that thank God for giving life to the dead, so can we move beyond literalist understandings of chosenness. Embracing the participation of "Jewish green card holders" in synagogue ritual life represents an American Jewish fulfillment of Isaiah's dream of a "house of prayer for all people" (56:7).

Such an embrace also provides a stinging counterpoint to the champions of the new atheism who caricature religious teachings and their adherents as xenophobic. The new atheists, primarily Christopher Hitchens and Richard Dawkins, have attracted growing popularity in the United States, as evidenced by a recent Pew Forum survey indicating that the fastest growing religious group in America are the unaffiliated who see religious teachings as "hypocritical, judgmental, and insincere." As a Reform Jew, however, I find their ideas utterly lacking in credibility or relevance. Hitchens and others divide the modalities of faith into either fundamentalism or atheism. In their worldview, one is either a closed-minded believer or an open-minded atheist. One is either primitive or modern, foolish or thoughtful. This either-or dichtomony presents no significant challenge to Jewish belief, since Jewish thought has always been characterized by a dialogical approach to matters of faith. Following the dictum that *eileh v'eileh divrei elohim chayim* (these and these are the words of the living God), the Sages frequently left debates over *agaddah*, over faith, unresolved. One could be a Jewish rationalist or Jewish mystic. Our tradition permits, even embraces, uncertainty.

Amidst this uncertainty, the foundation of faith that anchors every Jew is that of a covenant between him- or herself and God. The relationship between the individual Jew and God does not occur in a vacuum. The individual Jew is a member of the Jewish People, meaning that he or she is shaped by a history and tradition that makes demands on his or her thought and behavior. While the person has the right to dissent from covenantal practices and beliefs, he or she is not free from the duty to address them. Autonomy does not mean unlicensed freedom. Rather, it is a rejection of any notion of heteronomy and theonomy, and an embrace of partnership and existential freedom. It allows for flexibility, not ignorance, in a person's determination of the obligations of life within the covenant.

Spiritual Mappings

A Jewish Understanding of Religious Diversity

RABBI OR N. ROSE

SEVERAL YEARS AGO I had the privilege of interviewing my beloved teacher Rabbi Zalman Schachter-Shalomi, for the magazine *Tikkun*. Among the many stories Reb Zalman, a consummate storyteller, shared with me was about his experience studying with the distinguished African American preacher and writer Howard Thurman (1899–1981).

In the mid-1950s, after a decade of intensive training as a Chasidic rabbi in Brooklyn, Reb Zalman began, with some trepidation, to explore the academic study of religion at Boston University (BU), while serving as a congregational rabbi in a nearby suburb. At the outset of his time at BU, Reb Zalman's motto was "Wisdom among the nations, believe it. Torah among the nations, don't believe it" (*Lamentations Rabbah* 2:13), meaning, "I thought that the true spiritual treasures were among us

---

Rabbi Or N. Rose is an associate dean at the Rabbinical School of Hebrew College, and co-director of CIRCLE: The Center for Inter-religious and Communal Leadership Education, a joint venture of Andover Newton Theological School and Hebrew College. He is co-editor of *Righteous Indignation: A Jewish Call for Justice, God in All Moments: Spiritual and Practical Wisdom from Hasidic Masters*, and *Mysticism and the Spiritual Life: Classical Texts, Contemporary Reflections* (all from Jewish Lights). This essay is based, in part, on "In the Footsteps of Hillel: Judaism and Religious Pluralism," which appeared in *Tikkun* Magazine, November/December 2008.

Jews and even among Jews mostly with the Chasidim." Studying with Thurman, however, caused Reb Zalman to reconsider his religious worldview. He could no longer maintain his exclusivist theological stance in the face of this brilliant and soulful Christian teacher (whom he referred to as his "Black Rebbe"). Consequently, Reb Zalman's "reality map" began taking on a new pluralist shape. While remaining deeply immersed in Jewish life and practice, he began a lifelong study of the world's religions and an active, and now celebrated, practice of interfaith dialogue with religious leaders around the globe.

This story has served both as a catalyst and a challenge to me over the last few years. It has given me the confidence to engage more intensely in interfaith initiatives, and it has reminded me of the need to regularly unroll my "reality map" and revisit core questions of identity, belief, and observance in light of my interactions with people from other faith traditions. This chapter is my latest mapping exercise. Here I attempt to briefly sketch a theological approach to interfaith dialogue and action. It is my hope that this work-in-progress will be helpful to others engaged in, or considering engaging in, this sacred work.

Abiding the Mystery

Foundational to my understanding of life is the fact that all human knowledge is limited. This is true of matters secular and religious. Absolute truth is unavailable to any individual or community. The greatest of these mysteries for me, as a theologically oriented person, is God. While I have experienced what have felt like genuine encounters with the Divine—in nature, in conversation, and in prayer—I am left with more questions than answers. Is God a personal being, an impersonal force, or an ideal? Does God intervene in human affairs? Can human beings affect the Divine? Answers to these and other theological quandaries, I believe, should always be considered partial and unfinished.

One powerful articulation of this point is the medieval Jewish mystical notion of *ayin*, a description of God as "no-thing." This is not an atheistic statement, but an assertion about God's radical transcendence.

God is the One who surpasses all things—all thought and description. As the thirteenth-century German pietist Eleazar of Worms writes, "When you contemplate the Creator, realize that His encampment extends beyond ... in front, behind, east and west ... everywhere."[1] Translating this spatial metaphor, the kabbalists state that God is *Ein Sof* ("Infinity" or "The Infinite One"), beyond the limits of space and time, and, therefore, beyond human comprehension.

We can approach this unknowable deity, the mystics say, because God is also immanent, revealing something of Herself to us at all times. Our task is to open our eyes to the reality of the divine presence (*Shekhinah*) and to shape our lives around these moments of insight.

This paradoxical theological stance is expressed ingeniously in the opening pages of the *Zohar* (the masterwork of Kabbalah) in a reflection on the ancient Hebrew word *elohim*, the most common name for God in the Hebrew Bible. The *Zohar* authors deconstruct this name, reading it as two separate words: *mi* and *eileh*, "who" and "these." This wordplay reminds us of the precarious nature of theology: On the one hand, all we can say about God is *mi*: "Who are you? And what do you want of me?" On the other hand, we are given the freedom to engage imaginatively in God-talk: "*Eileh*, these are the ways in which I experience the Divine. And it is based on these encounters that I strive to shape my life." This dual message of mystery and insight remains as relevant today as it was for the medieval sages who articulated it centuries ago.

Human Interpretation

If I accept the reality of God's infinite nature and the limits of human knowledge, then I must also acknowledge that Judaism, like all other religions, is an imperfect attempt by my forebears to translate their spiritual experiences, beliefs, and values into a communal culture with specific religious symbols, rituals, spaces, and times. Abraham Joshua Heschel articulates this position powerfully in *God in Search of Man* when he states, "As a report about revelation, the Bible is itself midrash."[2] That is to say, even the texts we consider to be foundational to our religious traditions are products of human interpretation (midrash), and because they are the work of finite beings, they are necessarily imperfect. While the Hebrew Bible and other Jewish canonical sources are profound religious works, perhaps even divinely inspired, they are not the unmediated words of God.

As one who views the Hebrew Bible as an edited work, produced by various writers over many generations, I recognize within the *Tanakh* differences of opinion on matters large and small. As John Levenson notes in *Ethnicity and the Bible*, "The Bible is an anthology of writings composed over a period of about a thousand years, in several lands, by authors of different sorts."[3] And these authors disagreed about many issues, including such fundamental matters as the creation of humankind, the revelation at Sinai, and the messianic future.

Just as our ancient forebears held divergent views, so it is with each and every interpreter of Torah and other sacred texts. This hermeneutical principle is captured dramatically in the rabbinic statement "Just as the hammer splits the rock into many splinters, so will a scriptural verse yield many meanings" (BT *Sanhedrin* 34a, based on Jeremiah 23:29). As David Stern comments in *The Jewish Study Bible*, "It is often remarked that what is Jewish about the Bible is not the Bible itself, or even the Hebrew text of the Bible, but the interpretation of the Bible."[4]

It is this appreciation of the plurality of human interpretation that leads the early Rabbis to record majority and minority opinions on every page of the Talmud. Though Hillel may be deemed the winner of nine out of ten debates, Shammai's opinions are always recorded alongside those of his chief interlocutor.

> Rabbi Abba stated in the name of Samuel: For three years there was a dispute between the School of Shammai and the School of Hillel.... Then a Heavenly Voice announced, "The utterances of both are the words of the living God."
> (BT *Eiruvin* 13b)

Not only are Shammai's rulings considered sacred—"words of the living God"—but later mystics assert that his judgments will become law in the messianic age. This does not mean that we cannot take strong positions on a range of issues (after all, the Rabbis in our text argue for three years!), but our Sages instruct us to do so with an appropriate measure of humility, knowing that God's truth is infinitely more complex than we can fathom.

A Partnership Perspective

The dialogical approach of the early Rabbis can serve as an important model for interfaith relations, even if the Rabbis of the past could not envision it as such. Just as the Sages engaged in impassioned discussions about the nature and meaning of life, so too can people of different religious communities. The goal of such conversation is not unanimity, but a respectful exchange in which individuals learn from one another, critique one another, and agree to disagree about matters of substance.

The importance of engaging respectfully in these sacred deliberations is spoken of in the continuation of the talmudic text quoted above:

> Since both are the words of the living God, what was it that entitled the School of Hillel to have the law fixed according to them? Because they were kindly and modest, they studied their own rulings and those of the School of Shammai, and they [were even so humble as to] mention the opinions of the School of Shammai before theirs. (BT *Eiruvin* 13b)

Given the tragic history of religious disputation, this insight is particularly significant for contemporary interfaith dialogue.

Religious seekers are wise to heed Irving Greenberg's call in *For the Sake of Heaven and Earth* for the development of a "partnership perspective" in which we actively participate in shared interfaith learning experiences, knowing that each community has developed ideas and practices that can be beneficial to others. Through such encounters we have the opportunity to explore various themes that are absent from or occupy a minor role in our tradition and ask how these ideas might challenge and deepen our religious lives and help better the world.

In truth, religious communities have been borrowing from one another for centuries, consciously or not. Judaism would have lost its vitality long ago had our leaders not creatively adapted various concepts and practices from other religions and philosophical systems. Unlike earlier moments in our history, however, Jews now have the freedom and security to openly discuss the dynamic interaction of religions with dialogue partners from other faith communities.

The Non-Jew in Classical Jewish Literature

While I have drawn on a number of ancient and medieval Jewish sources to construct my argument, one can certainly find many derogatory statements about non-Jews and non-Jewish spiritual traditions in classical Jewish literature. This negativity is attributable to a number of factors, including doctrinal differences, human competition, and our ancestors' repeated experiences of persecution—physical and spiritual—at the hands of other nations. Yet, several traditional rabbinic authorities agree that non-Jews are capable of living decent and upright lives without taking on the yoke of the Jewish tradition. This is articulated most famously in the seven Noahide laws (JT *Avodah Zarah* 8:4), a brief list of moral norms created by the early Rabbis. It is this same line of reasoning that leads to the talmudic statement "The righteous of all nations have a share in the world-to-come" (BT *Sanhedrin* 8b).

The fact remains, however, that past Jewish thinkers regularly spoke of the Jewish People as God's chosen people and of Judaism as the highest form of religious service. These two claims are woven together tightly in an early rabbinic text (*Pirkei Avot* 3:18) attributed to the great sage and martyr Rabbi Akiva. The teaching opens with the statement that all people are created in the divine image (Genesis 9:6) and that God loves all of humankind. However, it goes on to say that only the people of Israel are considered God's children. Further, the Divine Parent gives these offspring the ultimate gift, Torah, the finest set of teachings ever revealed by God to humankind.

Is God's love for Israel a more intense love than God's love for the nations of the world? Is the Jewish tradition—Torah writ large—a superior religious system to all others? Both of these questions need to be addressed if one is to engage in serious interfaith conversation.

Chosen or Choosing?

In response to these claims, I must say that I do not believe that the Jewish People are God's chosen people and I do not consider Judaism superior to other religions. Simply put, I have learned too much from non-Jews and from non-Jewish religious and secular sources to uphold either of these positions. This does not mean that I consider all religious concepts and practices to be equally valid, but I do not think that Judaism is better than Christianity, Islam, or the great spiritual traditions of the East. Further, when I contemplate the issue of divine love, I would like to think that God loves all human beings equally—a feat beyond human capacity—and recognizes the unique value of each individual and community.

Having said that, Judaism is the primary context in which I choose to live my life. This has everything to do with the positive influence of my parents and siblings and a number of gifted teachers and mentors. Whether accidental or providential, Judaism continues to nurture and challenge me in my growth as a spiritual and ethical being, even as I wrestle with some of its foundational teachings. I feel blessed to be a part of such a rich religious and cultural tradition that continues to evolve thousands of years after its inception. As a rabbi, I am committed to working to preserve and renew the Jewish tradition, particularly in a time when many Jews are opting out of Jewish life. Further, I believe that Judaism has played a vital role in the development of Western culture and has significant contributions to make to the contemporary world.

In 1965, Abraham Joshua Heschel addressed the Protestant students and faculty of Union Theological Seminary with the following words:

> Parochialism has become untenable.... The religions of the world are no more self-sufficient, no more independent, no more isolated than individuals or nations.... Energies, experiences, and ideas that come to life outside the boundaries of a particular religion or all religions continue to challenge and to affect every religion. Horizons are wider, dangers are greater.... No religion is an island.[5]

The power of Heschel's statement has only grown in the intervening decades. Globalization has brought with it unprecedented opportunities for communication and cooperation, as well as for violence and destruction. This makes the need for constructive interfaith dialogue and action more urgently needed than ever before. This is especially so given that some extremist religious groups are using the technological instruments of this new century to spread messages of intolerance and hatred and to commit atrocities in the name of God.

It is crucial, therefore, for religious people who oppose such expressions of religion to articulate alternative narratives—narratives that encourage respectful interfaith and cross-cultural engagement. This reflection is but one attempt at doing so. I encourage others to add their voices to the conversation, expressing their own theological perspectives, drawing their own spiritual maps. As Heschel said, "Horizons are wider, dangers are greater."[6] The question is whether or not religious communities can build the necessary bridges to heal past wounds and help create a more just and compassionate world. The choice is ours; let us choose wisely.

The Religion of Torah

Benjamin D. Sommer, PhD

LET ME BEGIN at the beginning, at Sinai. This first sentence already intimates an answer to the first question posed to us: revelation is the pivot of my Jewish identity. There are other points one might have designated as the beginning of the Jewish People: the election of Abraham, his migration together with Sarah and members of his extended family to what would become the Land of Israel, the transformation of their descendants into a nation in the crucible of Pharaoh's persecution, or their liberation from slavery. But Rabbi Isaac in *Midrash Tanchuma* and Rashi in his commentary to Genesis 1:1 are correct when they say that all of Genesis and the first part of Exodus are a preface to the main event of Torah, which is the revelation of law. Even the Exodus was not the true beginning, for God took us out Egypt for a purpose: so that Israel might receive the law at Sinai and then continue to their own land where they would build a society based on it. God did not tell Pharaoh, "Let

Benjamin D. Sommer, PhD, is professor of Bible and ancient Semitic languages at The Jewish Theological Seminary. Previously, he served as director of the Crown Family Center for Jewish Studies at Northwestern University and as a visiting faculty member at Hebrew University and the Shalom Hartman Institute. He is currently working on the Jewish Publication Society commentary on the book of Psalms. His first book, *A Prophet Reads Scripture: Allusion in Isaiah 40–66*, was awarded the Salo Wittmayer Baron Prize by the American Academy for Jewish Research. His second book, *The Bodies of God and the World of Ancient Israel*, received the Jeremy Schnitzer Prize from the Association of Jewish Studies.

My people go, because freedom is a good thing," but "Let My people go, so that they may serve Me" (Exodus 7:16, 7:26, 8:16, 9:1, 9:13, 10:3).

Redemption from slavery carries little value on its own in Torah, which does not find the notion of Israel's slavery inherently bothersome. Torah is concerned, rather, with the question of whom the slaves serve, and how. "It is to Me that the Israelites are slaves: they are My slaves, whom I freed from the land of Egypt" (Leviticus 25:55); and Torah presents the duties of that exalted slavery when it describes what happened at Sinai.

The Jewish liturgy says repeatedly, God gave Torah to the Jewish People; the wisdom tractate of the Mishnah, *Pirkei Avot*, begins, "Moses received Torah at Sinai and passed it on," which is to say, made it a tradition. But what do these crucial verbs—God gave, Israel received—mean? The authority of Jewish law and the sacred status of the Bible rest on these verbs, and thus thinking carefully about them is of the greatest significance.

I align myself with the stream of modern Jewish thought that regards the revelation as a real event in history in which God made God's commanding presence known to Israel. For this stream of thought, this event did not necessarily involve any specific words. Revelation was nothing less and nothing more than God's command to Israel. The specific laws of the Torah record Israel's response. The text we find in the Five Books of Moses is not God's creation; it records Israel's attempts to flesh out what God requires. This reaction to and explication of God's voice at Sinai continue throughout Jewish history, for, as several midrashim on the phrase *kol gadol v'lo yasaf* in Deuteronomy 5:19 teach, God's voice at Sinai was "a great voice that never stopped." It speaks to all Jews at all times and places. Other midrashim express this same idea by saying that all of us stood at Sinai. The opening verses of Deuteronomy 5 already hint at this idea when they describe Moses as telling the Israelites shortly before they crossed into the Promised Land, "It was not with our fathers that God made this covenant, but with us, the living, every one of us who is here today" (Deuteronomy 5:3), even though the generation that had literally stood at Sinai had died off during the preceding forty years in the wilderness. Since God's voice continues speaking to us, our response continues as well.

The Mishnah, the Gemara, medieval philosophical, mystical, and halakhic literature—all of these are part of the Jewish People's ongoing reaction. The book you are reading right now aspires to be part of that response, as do halakhic rulings made in the past few years, whether they are concerned with legumes on Passover or homosexuality. All of these are attempts to hear God's voice at Sinai more clearly, to extend its reach, to apply it to the present day.

The ideas about revelation I am endorsing are not my own creation; they have been articulated especially well by thinkers such as Franz Rosenzweig, Abraham Joshua Heschel, and Louis Jacobs, and they have forebears going back through medieval and rabbinic literature into the Bible itself. I need not detail them here. Instead, I would like to note an overlooked implication of this theory of revelation as it pertains to the rabbinic doctrine of the two Torahs. A bedrock teaching of rabbinic Judaism is that God gave us two Torahs at Sinai: the Written Torah, which consists of the Bible, and the Oral Torah, which was passed on orally and eventually written down in the various works of rabbinic literature. While both Torahs are authoritative and sacred, they differ in two crucial respects.

First, the Written Torah is fixed and unchanging. It consists of the Masoretic text of the twenty-four books that make up the *Tanakh*, or Bible. The Oral Torah is not as fixed. It consists not only of the classical works of rabbinic literature dating to the first millennium CE but also of more recent works, even, potentially, teachings of our own day and of the future. As a result, the boundaries of Oral Torah are somewhat vague: The Mishnah is clearly in, while *Masechet Sof'rim* (an extra-canonical tractate sometimes published along with but not quite as a part of the Talmud) lies near the border, perhaps on the outer side. Both the Jerusalem Talmud and the *Nefesh Hachayim* (a nineteenth-century scholastic work) are definitely in, but the former is somehow more in than the latter.

Second, while the Rabbis regard the Oral Torah as sacred, authoritative, and in some respect divine in origin, the Rabbis also recognize that the Oral Torah contains a substantial human element. As our teachers starting with Moses and Joshua passed the Oral Torah on, they augmented it, forgot parts of it, interpreted it, and at times misinterpreted it. Oral Torah mixes divine elements revealed at Sinai with human elements, and these human elements are not perfect. It follows that Judaism knows of a category of religious writing that is at once holy and flawed.

Now, for those of us who regard the Bible as Israel's reaction to divine revelation (or, as Heschel famously put it, a midrash on revelation), it seems clear that the Written Torah is another sort of Oral Torah. Even the Pentateuch is a human formulation that responds to revelation, and hence it is tentative and groping rather than definitive. The Pentateuch is one of many human interpretations of divine self-disclosure to Israel, as are the midrashic collections, medieval commentaries, and modern scholarly works, not to mention questions asked last Saturday morning by a worshiper at a synagogue's Torah discussion. The modern approach to revelation compels us to state (even though neither Heschel nor Rosenzweig acknowledged this corollary of their own thought): there really is no Written Torah; there is only Oral Torah, which starts with Genesis 1:1.

Some Jews might be fearful of this corollary, regarding it as harmful or threatening to Jewish belief, since it seems to deflate the claim of scripture to be sacred or other-worldly. But I think it is constructive and helpful for several reasons. First, from the point of view of rabbinic Judaism, this suggestion is less radical than it might sound. Many rabbinic texts tell us that the Written Torah is really a subset of the Oral Torah, or that they overlap quite substantially, or that the line dividing them is coincidental rather than essential. (I think here of texts like *Exodus Rabbah* 47:1, *Sifrei Deuteronomy* 306, BT *Gittin* 60a–b, JT *Pe'ah* 2:6, and their many parallels.) Second, I think this corollary takes the sting out of many of the findings of modern biblical scholars and theologians. Rabbinic Judaism has long had a notion of a text that is holy and authoritative, yet also human and imperfect. It is no contradiction for a religious Jew to say, "I regard the Pentateuch as sacred because it represents my people's first response to God's voice at Sinai, and I regard that response as compelling, central to my life, and, at times, flawed." We have always said that about Oral Torah, and we do not endanger our faith if we recognize the same set of characteristics in Written Torah. It follows that later Jewish authorities can make their own additions to our tradition. They can even alter the tradition when truly necessary. Indeed, it is clear that throughout Jewish history, they have done so—at times to a greater extent, usually to a lesser one.

The command comes from God. But the specifics of the law have always been human in origin, and hence it is no surprise that the Jewish People at times modify them. Now, what I state in the second of the two preceding sentences is, outside of Orthodoxy, a widespread idea in recent Jewish thought, which emphasizes the organic and changing nature of Halakhah. What needs to be stressed is the first sentence: the command that lies behind the specific laws comes from God. The covenant formed at Sinai is mutual and dialogical. But the Bible and rabbinic literature make very clear that it is not a contract between equals. There is a Master and there are slaves. We are the slaves. As the great Jewish thinker Yeshayahu Leibowitz has emphasized, to be a religious Jew, one must accept this hierarchical structure, whether one likes it or not. Modern Jews (and I am excluding most Orthodox Jews from this category) have eagerly embraced the dialogical nature of the covenant; we are comfortable, indeed delighted, with the notion that we are God's partners. We have failed, however, to acknowledge the covenant's hierarchical side and consequently we cannot claim to have fully embraced this covenant.

Let me spell out a few implications of the side of the covenant we modern Jews have lost. It is possible for Jews to change the tradition that stems from Sinai, but we can only do so in fear and in trembling. God gave us the awesome responsibility of interpreting and applying God's command. Doing so cannot be an exercise in shaping the tradition in our own image, in making it hew to our predilections. We modern Jews claim, I think rightly, that some laws in the tradition result from a misunderstanding of what the merciful and just God wants—for example, the command to kill Amalekite babies. Just as our ancestors and forebears in ancient Israel erred terribly when they responded to Sinai by authoring this law in Exodus 17 and Deuteronomy 25, so too is it possible that we are sometimes mistaken as we attempt to apply God's command to our time.

If revelation is a dialogue, then I need to recall that in a dialogue, mine is not the only voice. Participating in any dialogue requires one to be still and listen—how much the more so in a dialogue in which we are mere vassals! Part of our job in our Sinaitic dialogue is to be silent in God's presence, so that we can be open to God's voice and also to the voices of the generations of servants who came before us. (The Conservative movement has long proclaimed as its motto "Tradition and Change." It needs to recall that in this motto there is a word before the "and.") As I think about our need to respect tradition, I find many statements of contemporary Jewish thinkers odd, and at times pointless. "I don't believe in the reinstitution of sacrifices," I have heard teachers, colleagues, and students state more times than I care to count. The only valid response I can think of to such a statement is, Who cares? What difference does it make what you or I think about sacrificing animals? When the messiah arrives, he or she will inform us, with the highest degree of authority, what the arrangements are going to be in the rebuilt Temple, and then our role will be to implement them. Since none of us today is a prophet, making predictions about what will happen in the messianic era is foolish; emoting about what we want to happen then is more than a little narcissistic. Speaking of the messiah, I confess that the whole notion of a messianic era is problematic to me personally. I mention this not because it matters but to point out that my problems with this notion do not matter at all. When I recite the *Amidah*, it is not my job to censor out the many references to the end of days it contains but to grapple with them and to attempt more fully to accept what they say. (Of course, in doing so, I am aided by the knowledge that already in the Bible, and also in rabbinic literature, authoritative Jewish teachers debate the exact contours of this concept, though none of them rejects it.)

I am not claiming, of course, that the limits of Jewish belief are so severe that our role is simply to accept doctrine without thinking. The richly varied nature of Jewish tradition makes doing so impossible and inauthentic. But Judaism's love of debate and discussion, of *machloket* and *shakla v'tarya*, should not lead us to the false conclusion that any opinion is legitimate. For example, there are surprisingly diverse ideas on the nature of God in the Bible itself, in rabbinic literature, and among medieval Jewish philosophers and mystics. But no classical Jewish thinker accepts the idea that there is more than one God or less than one. To claim that there can be such a thing as a polytheistic Judaism or an atheistic Judaism is intellectually dishonest and religiously obscene. Our own preferences and needs can never be the benchmark for accepting or rejecting a belief or practice. To be religious means, among other things, to be humble, and humility is sorely lacking in the ways that modern Jews appropriate tradition. This doesn't mean we should stop appropriating, applying, and reshaping the tradition, but it does mean we need to do so with a greater sense of awe and a greater realization of how small and insignificant we are. While the limits on Jewish belief are hard to identify, the humility that is a prerequisite for participating in the ongoing conversation that is Torah requires us to acknowledge that they do exist, even if we are not positive where they are.

I pointed out above that Oral Torah is not fixed but grows in every generation. I have gone on to point out, nonetheless, that not every idea expressed by a Jew is Torah. Some interpretations, legal rulings, and theological teachings are out of bounds. How can we tell which teachings are part of Oral Torah and which are not? The answer is quite simple. Come back in five hundred years and look around. What are religious Jews doing? What are they studying? What shapes who they are? That is Torah. Which contributions of twenty-first-century Jews have they forgotten? Which ones have they discarded? Which ones have they never even heard of? That is not Torah. In the year 50 CE, there was no theoretical criterion that allowed a person to say which forms of Judaism were the right ones. On a purely intellectual level nobody could claim that the traditions of the Pharisees and the earliest

Rabbis were Torah, while the writings of the Qumran sect and the teachings of the Sadducees were not. But by the year 600, it was clear that this was the case. There is no definitive way to explain why the philosopher Philo's first-century attempt to fuse Plato and Judaism did not become Torah, while Maimonides' twelfth-century attempt to fuse Aristotle and Judaism did; but there is no denying that Philo's writings (which were not preserved by Jews but came down to us because they were copied by Christian clerics) are not Torah, while Maimonides' books (in spite of all the opposition to them during his lifetime) have become the most revered and widely studied works of the post-talmudic era. This answer seems unsatisfying to some people. They want to know now who is right, the Orthodox or the Conservative, this halakhic ruling or that. But here again we see the narcissism that infects modern Jewish thinking. There is Torah, and some of what we teach today will become part of it. What difference does it make that we ourselves won't live to see which ideas and rulings they are? Our task is only to nurture, protect, and create Torah with as much honesty as possible, and to live that Torah, to teach it, and to pass it on. We cannot complete that task, but we are not free to desist from it. In order to fulfill our obligation, we need to stand, every morning and evening, at Sinai; there we must, again and again, acknowledge God's sovereignty and accept God's command.

WAYS OF
TALKING
ABOUT GOD

Five Pillars of Orthodox Judaism

Rabbi Asher Lopatin

NOT LONG AGO, I was sitting on a plane with a wonderful man who was a Satmar Chasid. The Satmar Chasidim live in a few, tight-knit communities in America and Israel and are known as being beyond ultra-Orthodox—they are seen as "petra-Orthodox." They dress religiously—black and white—they speak religiously—Yiddish—and they read religiously—only approved books and censored Internet. They are passionate about, and committed to, a type of Judaism that shuns as much of the Western world as possible. We had several hours of great conversation on a long flight, and the contrast to my modern Orthodox life reinforced my need to examine once again who I was, what I was passionate about, and what kind of Judaism I was committed to. Was my modern Orthodox lifestyle, which embraces and engages the Western world while still clinging to the details of traditional Jewish law and practice, less religious than his? Was my Judaism a watered-down or compromised version of his?

Rabbi Asher Lopatin is the rabbi of Anshe Sholom B'nai Israel Congregation, a modern Orthodox synagogue in Chicago. He was selected by *Newsweek* magazine as one of the twenty-five top American pulpit rabbis. Prior to the rabbinate, he studied Islam at Oxford on a Rhodes scholarship. He is married to Rachel Tessler Lopatin, and they have four children.

Actually, I have pondered these questions over the years, especially since becoming a rabbi of a modern Orthodox synagogue over a decade ago. The longer I ponder, the more I think that the Judaism that I have adopted for my way of life, and hopefully for my family's way of life, is not only authentic but essential for the well-being of Judaism. For Judaism to thrive, it needs modern Orthodoxy. In fact, I would argue that of all the types of Orthodoxy, I believe modern Orthodoxy is the ideal form. Labels are limiting and off-putting, but Orthodoxy is more of a brand name than just a label; I wish to sincerely define the brand name of Orthodoxy in a way that will make my modern Orthodox brothers and sisters proud to be modern Orthodox, not ashamed that they are not as good as the ultra-petra-Orthodox up the street or in the other part of town.

Yet while it is important to realize that modern Orthodoxy may be what Orthodoxy was meant to be, it cannot rest on its laurels. In fact, it is the most delicate form of Orthodoxy. Engaging in the world around us, trying to take the good and stay away from the bad, is difficult. All the wonders that modern Orthodoxy provides can fall apart if modern Orthodox Jews do not take their own religion seriously. Ultra-Orthodox Jews seem to do a good job taking Judaism seriously; modern Orthodox Jews need to do the same. There is joy and love for the religiously committed Jew, but to make Orthodox Judaism work, it has to be *r'tzini* (serious) at its core.

The Five Pillars

A few years ago I came up with five pillars of Orthodox Judaism. They are not principles of faith; I have left that to Maimonides, the fifteenth-century philosopher Joseph Albo, and others who have worked on that years ago. These are the foundations that should help make someone committed to modern Orthodoxy aware of what his or her faith and way of life is based upon and also alert him or her to the passion that that life is based on.

1. Torah Mi'Sinai—*Torah from Sinai*

Both the Oral and Written Torah come from God and were revealed to the Jewish People at Sinai. In contrast to the great Conservative halakhist Rabbi Joel Roth, who said, "Halakhic tradition is the given, and theology is required to fall into place behind it,"[1] I believe our halakhic tradition needs to be driven by theology in order to keep Judaism alive and infinite, rather than ossified and limited. We need to start with awe of the Torah and Talmud coming from God, being infinite and deserving infinite reverence. We need to place ourselves humbly below it, and only then establish ownership of it and make it our "plaything," as King David says in Psalms (119). Only when a couple accepts *kiddushin* (betrothal) can they become intimate with each other, and our Rabbis compare *matan Torah* (receiving Torah) to *kiddushin*. Only if you feel Torah is your God-given partner can you then become intimate with her. Only then can you really feel you are so connected to Torah that you can make a conjecture as to what she is thinking; only then you can trust your instincts in interpreting Torah's 3,500-year tradition. This theology and intimacy leads to the second pillar.

2. Chidush Mi'Sinai—*Innovation from Sinai*

New understandings and innovative interpretations come if you believe Torah is divine and infinite and, thus, can be interpreted in an infinite amount of ways. If you are truly *chareid* (fearful, awestruck) of *d'var Hashem* (the word of God), then you can never have the audacity, the *chutzpah*, to believe that you or any human being can truly know what that word of God means. You can never say something is "clear from Torah." How can the divine word of God, communicated to mere mortals, ever be clear, easy to understand, or obvious? Any new interpretation must be processed and examined through the traditions of *p'sak* (rulings) of the last two thousand years, and that interpretation must follow the Talmud. And yet, we may re-read the Talmud in a totally different way without changing the eternal Torah of God that the Talmud represents. Our re-reading will be debated, resisted, and challenged, but, ultimately, if it is a real interpretation of the Talmud—as far as can be humanly established—and it fits into the understanding of Rishonim (medieval authorities) and the subsequent authorities, it will become part of *Halakhah l'Moshe mi'Sinai*—the Halakhah that was understood to have been given to Moses at Sinai, even if Moses never understood it the way someone in the twenty-first century understands the word of God. Innovation comes from the dialectic of ideas from the world around us and our allegiance to Torah, the eternal, infinite word of God. Within this dialectic, *chidushim*, innovative ways of understanding our Torah and tradition, arise in every generation.

3. Halakhic Rigor and Discipline

When we closely observe our detailed laws of *kashrut*, davening, coming to minyan and making sure there is a minyan in our communities, *kavvanah* (concentration, focus) in our davening, Shabbat as it is expressed in its myriad rituals and ethical aspects, family purity in its own ritual and social aspects, the laws of gossiping and loving our fellow Jews and respecting our fellow human beings, then we become worthy vessels through which Torah can be interpreted and even rethought. The Netziv put it in terms of two words: *ushmartem va'asitem*, "Preserve and do" (Deuteronomy 4:6). We need to first be the preservers of Torah who inherit from the previous generation; then we can move on to doing, relooking at everything with fresh, innovative eyes to understand Torah for our generation. When we are preservers of Torah and Torah practice, then we become safe space for God's infinite word. We become the rightful heirs of the tradition, which we are obliged to re-examine for ourselves. Only through this rigor and commitment to Halakhah, *minhag* (custom), and tradition can our lives reflect the living Torah that God gave us at Sinai.

4. Klal Yisrael: *Inclusivity*

Yisrael, oraita v'kudshah b'rich hu echad hem, "Israel, the Torah, and God are all one." If one of them is disrespected, the other one suffers. How can a person who doesn't feel *Yisrael mi'Sinai*—that the loving and caring relationship between all Jews is a requirement from God—really believe in *Torah mi'Sinai*? If a person cannot respect the yearnings of Jewish women or the feel the pain of a patrilineal Jewish teenager who is told that they were never really Jewish to begin with, then that person is rejecting *echad hem*, the unity of *Yisrael mi'Sinai*, *Torah mi'Sinai*, and the belief in our being connected to the one and only God. And beyond a respect for the family, for Jews, with whom we are bonded together with God, there is the fifth principle, which pushes us to look not just inside, but outside as well, with concern for all those created in God's image.

5. Menchlichkeit *and* Kiddush Hashem: *Always Asking Yourself, Am I Acting Like a Mensch?*

Am I acting with respect to all of God's creations? Am I seeing God in every human being the way God wanted us to see the Divine in every descendant of Adam and Eve? Finally, am I acting in such a way as to allow decent people to see God in me? Orthodox Judaism does have a universalistic tendency to see the *tzelem elohim* (image of God) in every human being and to act through *tzelem elohim* in this world—to be human and humane. *V'rachamav al kol ma'asav*, "God's mercy extends to all of God's creatures" (Psalms 145).

Coke Classic

Modern Orthodoxy is "Coke Classic," not "New Coke" as many think. Coke Classic still may taste different to different people in different times. And Coke Classic needs to maintain a high level of quality control, otherwise it will be replaced by Pepsi or, worse, distilled water! Coke Classic is the standard by which all other flavored, fizzy drinks are judged, just as modern Orthodoxy can be that standard, with an infinite amount of subflavors. Modern Orthodoxy can sing the infinite word of God "in perfect harmony" from the generation of Sinai until the end of time.

Toward a New Jewish Theological Lexicon

Rabbi Michael Marmur, PhD

FOR MANY, certain ways of talking about God, Torah, and Israel are impossible or irrelevant. Some of us are in search of a new way of expressing our sense of commitment and responsibility, our yearnings and principles. Rather than repeat big statements about sin and virtue, we are in search of syntax and vocabulary. Canadian philosopher Charles Taylor recently coined the term *social imaginary* to describe ways in which large groups of people imagine their surroundings: the images, stories, and legends they use to express the world they inhabit. He argues that it is this social imaginary that make possible common practices. New thinking about Judaism may be less about the formulation of ready-to-wear axioms, and more about the terms, key concepts, and images that will provide the raw material for something new to take shape.

I want to present three concepts that, for me, merit a place in a new Jewish theology, which remains unwritten. It is no coincidence that all of these terms are from the Hebrew language. I firmly believe that the revival of Hebrew in our times will have a profound cultural and reli-

Rabbi Michael Marmur, PhD, is assistant professor of Jewish theology and vice president for academic affairs at Hebrew Union College–Jewish Institute of Religion (HUC–JIR). He served for over ten years as dean of HUC–JIR's Jerusalem School, and he is still based there. He specializes in the thought of Abraham Joshua Heschel.

gious impact on future generations. These words are written, ironically enough, in English, and much Jewish thought has been generated in languages other than that of the Bible. But Hebrew has usually been crucial in the creation of new theological languages, and we are living in an era of unprecedented Hebrew creativity. A new Jewish theology should read from right to left, and from left to right. Tomorrow's Jewish social imaginary is likely to be a two-way street.

Neder: A Vow Freely Made

I am a modern liberal Jew. For me, the prospect of abandoning Judaism is inconceivable: I strive to live a rich and intense Jewish life. I find it neither plausible, possible, or necessary to express this commitment by taking on a traditional halakhic lifestyle. It is not plausible because the claims to exclusivity and ultimate authenticity made by contemporary exponents of Halakhah do not persuade me. It is not possible because a number of the social and cultural assumptions of this traditional halakhic approach are hard for me to bear. And it is not necessary to assume that only by engaging in metaphysical acrobatics and legal fictions can I make a meaningful Jewish life.

Thus far my liberal manifesto. But I have a problem believing that a vigorous Jewish life can be attained for individuals and in community without some Halakhah in its broadest sense: Halakhah as law, form, lifestyle, precision, argumentation, debate, praxis. This term should always be seen alongside its partner and counterpart, *aggadah*, denoting interpretation, inwardness, narrative, speculation, poetry. There is a beautiful and important essay by Haim Nahman Bialik in which the relationship between Halakhah and *aggadah* is described in these broad terms: "Halakhah without *aggadah* is dead. *Aggadah* without Halakhah is wild." Now, Bialik did not have in mind a small definition of these terms. Rather, he was talking about the interplay of two key life forces.

I agree with Bialik. Despite all my rejection of a traditional halakhic approach as implausible, impossible, and unnecessary, I am alarmed at the prospect of an unanchored liberal Jewish sensibility floating on the seas of contemporary life and being tossed about by the waves. I am convinced that without some Jewish praxis, some way or ways of doing things and being in the world, we are left with lofty pronouncements that sound more significant than they really are.

What should liberals who strive for a theology of Jewish commitment do? One way to begin is to reclaim and, of course, reinterpret the traditional term *neder*. *Neder* is a vow I make freely. Once I have made it, however, my words have consequences. My private commitment takes on a communal resonance. In the Bible, a husband or a father can cancel a woman's *neder*, so a discussion of the term also involves an examination of power relations and an understanding of human dignity.

I see myself as commanded in general terms to seek out ways of being good and holy in the world. Brought up in a certain household with certain norms and practices, I am heir to a heritage. Beyond these general and biographical dimensions, I am commanded to choose (and in a certain sense I choose to be commanded).

Let's be specific and practical: I may commit this year to rise every morning and pray, or to read a chapter of the *Tanakh*, or a tractate of the Mishnah. That is a specific expression of a general commitment, and I want to see it in terms of *neder*, a vow freely made. Now I would never want to see *neder* police, checking up on my performance. On the other hand, we live in communities of *n'darim*, where our commitments are pooled together. I believe that through time some of these commitments will stick and become part of our regular practice, and others will not. I even have a suggestion for when this moment of vowing may take place—the festival of Shavuot. That's when the Dead Sea Sectarians (not usually role models for liberal Jews) celebrated this festival as a renewal of the covenant, and I suggest we revive the practice. A celebration of Shavuot oaths, alongside the festival of Shavuot, counting the weeks from Exodus to revelation.

I want to live in a community in which personal commitments are taken with great seriousness and in which the communal and the personal intertwine. As a modern, I set great store by the need and the right of the individual person to find his or her own way, to make mistakes and discoveries. As a Jew, I seek a context in which this trial and error can have resonance beyond the confines of personal search. It may be that in the coming generation our discussion of *mitzvot* will have to involve a discussion of *n'darim*.

Middot: The Many Prisms for Understanding Torah

Jewish tradition knows of two great lists of thirteen *middot* (character traits). The word *middah* covers a variety of meanings, including measurement and virtue. The Rabbis identified a list of thirteen divine attributes based on Exodus 34:6–7:

> A God compassionate and gracious, slow to anger, abounding in kindness and faithfulness, extending in kindness to the thousandth generation, forgiving iniquity, transgression, and sin; yet He does not remit all punishment, but visits the iniquity of parents upon children and children's children, upon the third and fourth generations.

The second list of thirteen *middot* is attributed to the great sage Rabbi Ishmael, a contemporary of Rabbi Akiva. His list is often translated as a catalog of thirteen hermeneutical principles. Torah is not to be studied through one prism alone, neither must our approach be capricious or arbitrary. There are certain methods that can be applied and by which Torah can be understood.

My question is: what are the new *middot*, the new measures or principles or criteria or values by which Torah can be interpreted by us? A number of Rabbi Ishmael's thirteen hermeneutical principles deal with the categories known as *k'lal* and *p'rat*, the general and the particular. They apply specifically to biblical verses in which both general and specific legislation is included, but I read it in a broader sense: the way we read Torah depends on our capacity to hold both the individual and the collective in mind.

I have a few further suggestions for new *middot*: our Torah is read, for example, through the prism of science and reason. They are not deployed to prove or disprove the Torah, but rather as lenses through which we see the world. The founding fathers of Reform tended to believe that the application of science to Torah would yield the great non-metaphysical truths inherent in the biblical text. Marching toward progress like pilgrims, they believed that the shackles of superstition could be shaken off and a new world might be discovered. I am less convinced, but I do know that when I read Torah, I am influenced by the great "-ologies" of modernity, among them philology, archaeology, psychology, and more.

Another of the new *middot* is doubt. Rather than fight against it, it accompanies, challenges, and enriches my encounter with Torah. Doubt in its various manifestations is part of our baggage (or at least of mine), and I believe it can serve as a prism—the Rabbis called this visual device an *aspeklaria*—through which I receive Torah. It has always intrigued me that in seeking an etymology for this term Maimonides mentions the somewhat fanciful suggestion that *aspeklaria* comprises two words, *safeik r'iyah*, meaning something like "doubtful vision." Doubt is not only an obstruction to faith, it is a lens through which I encounter truth.

As an Israeli citizen, another *middah* that I employ in encounter with Torah is power. This dimension has been lacking for centuries, but for better and worse, it has returned. When in 1994 the late Baruch Goldstein read the last sections of the book of Esther and shortly after sprayed a mosque with bullets, he was providing a dreadful and perverse reading of an ironic text. His actions and the other realities of the Middle East require me to read my tradition with questions of power and sovereignty in mind. Now it is not only the acts of a homicidal maniac that bring the dimension of power to bear in my contemporary reading of Torah: such documents as the annual budget of the State of Israel and the ethical code of the Israeli Defense Forces have become significant expressions of our values (and of what remains to be achieved so that these values can be advanced).

The list goes on, but the gist of the idea is this: like Rabbi Ishmael in his day, we are enjoined to define and sharpen the tools we employ when we do Torah, when we read ourselves into and out from our tradition.

Shazuf: God Turns to Us

In modern Hebrew, the term used for *suntan* is taken from a root known to us in the Bible. The word's original sense, so it appears, is related to seeing, and a clue to the way in which an optical term came to be connected with tanning salons is to be found early in the Song of Songs. There we find the expression "The sun has gazed upon me" (1:6).

This metaphor is used to explain a swarthy complexion. Hebrew has changed remarkably little in three thousand years: when modern Israelis sunbathe, they use the same word King Solomon used on his vacations. There is, however, one significant difference. In the Hebrew spoken today, the verb is employed using the reflexive form, *l'hishtazeif*: literally, "I tan myself." While the ancients saw themselves as objects upon which the world and the worlds beyond this world act, we tend to see ourselves more as the subject than the object. We would rather look upon ourselves than consider the possibility that we are looked upon, which sounds intrusive and patronizing.

My belief in God includes the notion that we are not the eternal subject and that we are not only engaged in reflexive activity. The God in whom I believe turns to us, is in search for us, and in order to appreciate this I have to let go of the need to be constantly in charge and on top. I do not sun myself; the sun sees me. I do not simply reflect upon myself. God turns to me. Now I have to try to work out what that might mean. I have little in common with fundamentalists who are convinced that the details of this encounter are precisely definable. Indeed, I suspect that often this kind of faith is a convoluted form of reflexive sunbathing. I am much less confident about my ability to know what it is I am expected to do in response to God's interest. But I differ from my secular friends when they insist on seeing themselves the subject of every sentence. Look to the sun (carefully) and you may catch a glimpse of it staring at you.

There are several other terms that warrant a place in a new Jewish theology, and I hope to address some of them in the future. Among them is the term *ye'mamah*, a variant of the word denoting "day." Liberal Jews have tended to abandon the specifics of Jewish time in units smaller than a week. We are better at the Sabbath than we are at imbuing the rest of the week with sanctity and significance. I am in search of a Jewish praxis that rediscovers the day, the most basic and elemental unit of time distinction. But that term and others will like it will have to wait for a broader canvas.

In the meantime, here are my three terms relating to issues of commitment, tradition, and God-encounter: *neder*, *middot*, and *shazuf*. New languages of Jewish theological discourse are being created in many circles, and not just in theological tomes (of which there are few). There is much to be found in poetry, prose, and popular culture. There are general philosophers, literary theorists, Bible experts, and Talmud scholars asking Jewish theological questions. In time, a new language may take shape, a new Jewish social imaginary, or a number of them. Just imagine what a Jewish theology reflecting on the second half of the twentieth century might look like. Just imagine how this new language may sound when it is spoken from the heart.

Martin Buber

The Dialogue with God

RABBI WILLIAM PLEVAN

THERE IS A COMMON MISCONCEPTION that theology is about God. This is only partially correct. In truth, theology is about the relationship between God and God's creatures, particularly human beings. God's ultimate reality is a mystery, but writing theology does not mean claiming to know all the mysteries of the universe. Rather, the purpose of a theology is to consider how it is that human beings should live knowing that a loving God invites and commands us to partner in the act of creation. In this sense, Jewish theology is covenantal, it is about the joys and demands of living in a relationship with God. No modern Jewish thinker has done more to elaborate this approach to Jewish theology than Martin Buber, the twentieth-century translator, philosopher, socialist critic, and Zionist activist. The central idea of Buber's thought is that Judaism is about living in relationship, what he called dialogue, with God and with human beings. His thought has been enormously influential on Jewish and even Christian theologians, and his thought is indispensable for Jewish theology in our time. In what follows, I will present Buber's signature contributions to Jewish theology by examining his take on five

Rabbi William Plevan is a graduate of the Rabbinical School of The Jewish Theological Seminary and is currently a pursuing a doctorate in religion at Princeton University, where he is writing his dissertation on Martin Buber's philosophical anthropology. In addition to Jewish thought, his interests include interfaith dialogue, ethics, and political theory.

significant themes in Jewish theology: God's oneness, God's name, the image of God, good and evil, and holiness.

God's Oneness

For Buber, the greatest challenge to religious faith in the modern world is the rapid social, political, and technological changes that have characterized life in the West since about the seventeenth century, much of it done under conditions of violence and warfare. As modern people, and Jews in particular, we find ourselves at best in a world of constant flux and at worst suffering at the hands of those who take advantage of the shifts in power that come with such changes. He believed that Judaism and Jewish texts offer a unique set of teachings about humanity that can guide modern people to find ways to live meaningful lives under these conditions. Buber argued that the central teaching of the Jewish tradition is what he called "the dialogue with heaven," the idea that human beings can approach the one God, creator of the universe, at any time or place, and be heard.

Medieval Jewish theological traditions tended to emphasize God's remoteness from human beings. For medieval philosophers, God was the mysterious ground of being; for mystics, God could only be approached by those who knew the secrets of access to the divine splendor. Buber agreed that God can be mysterious, terrifying, and remote, but he also argued that the God Jews believe in is a God who is close, approachable, and responds to the call of humanity. The great religious models of the Bible—Abraham, Moses, Elijah, and Job—were all distinguished by their audacity in approaching God with their troubles and questions, even as they sought to obey and revere their God. In later generations, the early masters of the Chasidic movement recaptured this spiritual fire by finding sparks of holiness in the everyday piety of ordinary and unlearned Jews who called out to God in their joy and misfortune. Drawing on the prophetic idea of the "kingship of God" and the later Jewish hope for messianic redemption, Buber also argued that the Jewish People should work to create a universal community of human beings, not just Jews, that reflects and enacts God's love of creation, both human and non-human. Although he thought that such an ideal could not be achieved easily or rapidly, Buber believed that the instability and dislocation of modern social and family life could be overcome by a human community dedicated to living in dialogue with God.

Buber found this vision of interhuman and divine-human reconciliation in the *Sh'ma*, the biblical verse that has become the focal point of Jewish prayer: "Hear, O Israel, the Lord our God, the Lord is One" (Deuteronomy 6:4). For Buber, God's oneness is an assertion that the cosmos is a unified whole created by divine action. To believe in multiple deities who rival each other for power, as many ancient cultures did, is essentially to claim that the cosmos is fragmented; if the gods could not reconcile with each other, how could human beings, and how could human beings become reconciled with the cosmos that confronts them? The teaching that God is one means that the entire cosmos is subject to God's will, but is also the object of God's love. Every individual human being and every part of nature share the same parent, the same teacher, and the same judge. The belief in one God implies that there is one creation and one humanity, and the Jewish hope of a messiah and universal redemption of humanity is the belief that despite the seemingly endless human appetite for conflict, God and humanity can together bring harmony to creation.

The Divine Name

The idea that there is one God who creates all also implies that every moment and every place is an opportunity to encounter the divine presence, the *Shekhinah*. Buber beautifully expresses this idea in his translation and interpretation of the tetragrammaton, the four-letter name of God that Jews traditionally do not pronounce, transliterated as YHWH and commonly translated as "The Lord" or the "Eternal." In magical and mystical strands of Judaism, the name itself is considered a powerful force, and medieval philosophers like Maimonides interpreted the name to mean divine eternity. In his translation of the Bible, Buber drew on a different Jewish interpretive tradition, derived from the Midrash and Rashi, which understands the divine name in terms of the explanation God gives Moses at the burning bush in Exodus 3:14: "I will be what I will be." The divine name does not denote remoteness or eternality, but continued presence. "God will be" means, God will be with God's creatures in all times and places. As one Chasidic saying Buber was fond of goes: "Where is God? Wherever you let God in." God's promise to Moses, as to our ancestors before and to every Jew since, is that God is available to us when we cry out, in all our pain and degradation, and that God will be with us as we fight for justice, show loving-kindness to others, and move toward the light of redemption.

The Image of God

The Hebrew Bible expresses the idea of divine-human partnership with the notion that human beings are created in the image of God (Genesis 1:27). This is a bold statement that each and every human life is precious to God and that human dignity can never be compromised by any "greater good." It is also a statement of God's aspiration for humanity. Again, Buber draws on a rabbinic tradition in stating that the way for human beings to fulfill the promise of living in the divine image is to imitate divine action of love and caring for all creation. The Jewish ethical tradition provides not only rules and regulations but habits of character (*middot*) that model how human beings can imitate God's loving-kindness: visiting the sick, clothing the naked, and showing respect for the dead.

Above I noted that Buber's philosophy of Judaism centers on the idea of "the dialogue with heaven." Buber is probably best known, especially to non-Jewish scholars of religion, as a philosopher of dialogue. Separate from his writings on Judaism, Buber developed a philosophy of dialogue that reflected his interpretation of Judaism, even though most of his writings on dialogue do not mention Judaism explicitly.

Nonetheless, I think it is clear that Buber developed his philosophy of dialogue to teach how human beings can live in the divine image. In his most famous work, *I and Thou*, Buber delineates two primary ways human beings orient themselves toward others (not just people) in the world: I-You, translated by many scholars as I-Thou and thus became the English title for the book, and I-It. These two orientations manifest in relationships toward others: the I-You, or dialogical, orientation is characterized by openness and mutuality, whereas the I-It orientation is characterized by utility and formality. When I listen to a friend or play lovingly with my dog, I am exhibiting an I-You orientation because I am open and available to the other without limitation. This orientation has the characteristic of genuine dialogue in which both parties engage freely in conversation. When I use a horse to plow a field, however, even when I treat it humanely, or when I order food from a waiter in a restaurant, even if I leave a good tip, I am exhibiting an I-It orientation; my treatment of the other is defined and limited by specific roles we play and by benefits derived in the relationship. Reciprocity of a certain kind is characteristic of the I-It orientation, but only because both sides of the relationship gain something as the result of whatever arrangement defines the relationship.

Buber's philosophy of dialogue is a penetrating insight into the tensions of human life. We find ourselves following daily patterns, taking things and people for granted, but we yearn for a greater sense of connection. We want to awaken our spirit, but we know that for this to truly happen we need an encounter with something beyond ourselves. Buber believed that we cannot realize the possibility of humanity without connecting to the world in an I-You orientation. In the I-It orientation, we take care of business; in the I-You orientation we take care of our souls and those of others. Buber worried that modern life had become so preoccupied with the increased technical know-how due to industrial, scientific, and political developments and achievement that modern people were in danger of losing sight of the I-You orientation and losing their humanity in the process.

Good and Evil

I also think that Buber's idea of two orientations offers, as he intended it to, a very helpful philosophical account of two polarities central to the Jewish tradition: the polarity of good and evil inclinations, and the polarity of holy and profane. I will treat the good and evil inclinations first. Biblical commentators have noted that in Genesis 1, God proclaims that each act of creation is "good," except in the case of human beings. Human beings are not merely good, because they are implanted with free will and the ability to choose evil over good. Even though we are created in the divine image, we are also flesh and blood, flawed human beings who are often weak in the face of temptations to act selfishly and hurt others. Buber's notion of two orientations develops the rabbinic idea that human beings are created with two inclinations, the evil inclination (*yetzer hara*) and the good inclination (*yetzer hatov*). According to one oft-quoted rabbinic statement, without the evil inclination, a person would never build a house or get married. In this case, the word *evil* is not a great translation of what the Rabbis mean; what they mean is a self-regarding inclination, an inclination to do things for one's own survival and benefit, and for that of one's family and community. Buber did not understand the I-It orientation, this self-regarding inclination, to be inherently evil, but rather as a permanent feature of human existence that needed to be channeled, but not extirpated. The problem is when this inclination runs amok, cutting itself off from the I-You, other-regarding inclination. The forces of evil may appear in grand personae in history—the Hitlers, Pol Pots, and Osama Bin Ladens—but the tendency to ignore the needs of others is a feature of our daily lives and something we must confront within ourselves. What Buber's notion of the I-You orientation emphasizes is that real goodness involves genuinely recognizing the unique dignity of another person. Even though sometimes we act in the right way for less than noble reasons—to obey the rules, to gain honor or benefit—the achievement of truly good character involves recognizing how every person, animal, and thing is a creature of God and precious in God's eyes.

A Life of Holiness

To anchor ourselves in the other-regarding inclination is also to anchor ourselves in a life of holiness. The I-It orientation creates the realm of human action we call profane or secular (although this word has come to mean something else), the realm of action absent any consideration of what is holy or lofty. As with the evil inclination, we must pursue the profane ends of securing our livelihood and developing better technologies and skills to do so. No doubt these technologies and skills can be used to serve lofty ends, but that is only so, Buber would say, because of our sense of connection with God. In *I and Thou*, Buber suggests that the being we call God should be understood as the "Eternal You." All of our relationships in the I-You orientation direct us to the Eternal You. But this also means that while moments of isolation such as prayer offer opportunities to seek the divine presence, the essence of the religious life is the life of dialogue with all of creation. God is not found in isolation from the world, by leaving the world, but by living a holy life in the world.

Above, I said that for Buber, in the I-You orientation, we take care of the soul. It is crucial here that by "soul" I do not mean something that is distinct from the body. A major point of Buber's philosophy of Judaism is that in Judaism, holiness is not achieved by escaping the life of the body but by transforming the body into a vessel of holiness. In developing this point, Buber criticized two philosophical and cultural tendencies that I think remain with us. The first is a kind of spiritual escapism, which denies that there is any real lasting value to our bodily existence and sees this world as either a distraction from or a gateway to a higher spiritual reality. The second view glorifies the body and power and sees no higher life than the perfection of the body and the acquisition of power. The results of this way of thinking can be found in the pleasure-seeking ideal of consumerist culture (which may be an ideal to which almost no one actually subscribes but all of us confront daily), the profit-seeking ethos of corporatist culture, and the power-hunger of petty dictators and politicians. Buber argued that Judaism teaches that holiness is achieved when human beings turn their lives and their possessions into instruments of holiness, dedicating themselves to the service of God. This is how we can anchor the I-It orientation to the I-You orientation. We may have accumulated possessions, as most of us have done in our life time, in order to provide security and stability for ourselves and our families, to experience pleasure or attain social status and honor. But true honor comes from celebrating God's creation in a spirit of holiness, honoring something greater than ourselves, the God who created all that we have. Possessions are not an inherent obstacle to the life of holiness, and in fact, we can turn our possessions into instruments for living a holy life when we use them to serve compassion and justice.

Buber himself was an iconoclastic religious thinker who rejected the authority of rabbinic law (Halakhah) and proclaimed that religious ritual and standardized prayer were spiritually deadening and ultimately precluded the kind of direct relationship with God that is the hallmark of true Jewish piety. As a Conservative rabbi, committed to the value of traditional Jewish ritual practice, I have found that, despite himself, Buber has taught me a great deal about the meaning of the practices that I and other traditional Jews observe. Buber rejected the value of religious law because he thought that putting religious commitments in legal form would make these commitments into mere tools or skills. In a sense, Buber is correct about how religious law works, but I also think human beings need to have routines, tools, and skills that reflect their loftier aspirations so that when we go about our everyday lives, we are constantly confronted by the claims of the holiness that surrounds us. Thus, what Buber found problematic about law, I find extremely helpful in achieving the ends he himself proposed for Jewish religious life: finding holiness in everyday life.

The rituals of Jewish life—prayer, the Sabbath, dietary laws—are all ways of transforming the mundane into the holy. Buber thought that human beings could not live a fulfilling life without art, without the ability to creatively express the sense of holiness and wonder that confronts us in everyday objects. In a way, art is the culmination of our dialogue with human beings, God, and inanimate objects. If a person follows the patterns of Jewish ritual life with an awareness of the divine presence in our midst, then that person becomes, to borrow a phrase from Abraham Joshua Heschel, a living work of art. The commandments, laws, and rituals are just an artistic technique, but we can each provide a unique spirit to the way we engage in dialogue with God. As much as I value the law, I agree with Buber that the essence of religious life is how each individual becomes a holy vessel to serve the one God who longs for us to draw near, to heal us in our pain, and to celebrate with us in our joy.[1]

Radically Free and Radically Claimed

Toward the Next Stage of Liberal Jewish Theology

Rabbi Rachel Sabath Beit-Halachmi, PhD

The Blessing and Burden of Freedom

I am radically free. As a non-Orthodox modern Jew, I am ultimately religiously free to determine which rituals and commandments to observe, what prayers to say, and free to reinterpret, abandon, or even reclaim nearly any and all aspects of Jewish practice and belief. According to this liberal religious understanding of the covenantal relationship between God and the Jewish People, I am not a priori obligated to

Rachel Sabath Beit-Halachmi, PhD, is a rabbi and scholar who was ordained at Hebrew Union College–Jewish Institute of Religion and earned a PhD in Jewish philosophy at The Jewish Theological Seminary. She is the Shalom Hartman Institute's director of lay leadership education and co-director of its North American Scholars Circle. She is also a member of the faculty of HUC–JIR, Jerusalem, and teaches in communities throughout North America. She is co-author of two books, *Striving Toward Virtue* and *Preparing Your Heart for the High Holidays*, and author of many articles and rituals. She lives outside Jerusalem with her husband, Rabbi Ofer Sabath Beit-Halachmi, and their children, Tehillah and Yedidya.

observe all *mitzvot* of the Torah or to uphold all of the *mitzvot* established by the Rabbis according to how they have been interpreted by Orthodox Halakhah. I may be obligated to uphold those that relate to creating an ethical society and ethical relationships, but many commandments and rituals can no longer be deemed worthy of our adherence, usually for one of three reasons:

1. They do not lead to ethical outcomes, such as those laws that diminish the role of women in ritual life or leave women beholden to men who refuse to grant them a divorce.
2. They are not reflective of our contemporary attitude toward the non-Jew.
3. They appear to be irrelevant to the contemporary context.

Let me be clear, such a liberal attitude toward the commandments does mean that we are obligated to *study* all *mitzvot*, to learn about their origins and purposes. I may perform many of them and seek out new meaning for others, but I, the modern liberal Jewish woman, am taught that I need not—and perhaps should not—see myself as divinely commanded to perform all of them.[1]

This freedom, known in liberal Jewish thought as religious autonomy, is both a great gift of modern Jewish life and simultaneously a great burden. One of the many reasons it is such a gift is because of the many ways in which Judaism can evolve and embrace the ethical concerns of modernity, not the least of which is the equal religious status of Jewish women. But such freedom to allow a person's mind, heart, and soul (often described as conscience) to determine the nature of his or her religious life is indeed a "difficult freedom"[2] for two main reasons: (1) because it demands constant study and questioning with regard to the tradition; and (2) it often entails enormous complications in creating communal life and norms. I must first identify several of the underlying core problems of such a modern liberal stance before I can name and explain the pivotal elements of my Jewish theology, which might otherwise appear quite non-liberal or non-modern. I also must identify the new-old questions that I believe must be addressed in Jewish theology as a whole in light of the contemporary Jewish condition, including the complex realities of life in the State of Israel.

The Spiritual-Intellectual Tension of Modern Liberal Judaism: Autonomy and Authority

If I am free to choose how to live my Jewish life, how do I go about choosing as both an individual Jewish self and as a member of the collective people of Israel? Based on what sources of authority or knowledge do I make my autonomous Jewish decisions? Am I also free not to choose? Am I really completely free? Or, as I learn from my teacher, rabbi and theologian Eugene B. Borowitz, is my autonomy in fact limited because I am an "autonomous Jewish self," not just a universal self, and am thus covenanted with God and with the Jewish People, past, present, and future?[3] In other words, while I may be radically free— given my modern non-Orthodox situation—I am, in fact, simultaneously radically claimed both by God and by the Jewish People.[4] But how so? And for what purposes?

To be sure, a couple of centuries of liberal Jewish thought—from the rabbi-scholar Abraham Geiger, who helped establish Reform Judaism and its theology, to Borowitz, a leading liberal Jewish theologian of our day—have produced various responses to these foundational questions that emerge in non-Orthodox Jewish life given its particular tensions between authority and autonomy.[5] Nearly all of the attempts at establishing a liberal Jewish theology maintain several key ideas including the following:

1. The autonomy of the individual to choose
2. God as the idea of the ethical core of Judaism
3. The importance of both the universal and the particular, and thus a more open attitude toward the non-Jew
4. The centrality of the covenant with God; and, in time, as a product of its concern for ethics
5. The absolute value of religious equality for women

These principles, while attempting to resolve some of the core tensions of liberal Judaism, do not fully address the spiritual needs of our contemporary context. Today, four significant phenomena are occurring simultaneously, collectively creating the need to reconsider the above categories of liberal Jewish theology:

1. Greater ritual observance and creativity
2. An ever-broadening commitment to *tikkun olam* (repairing the world), which includes not merely social action but environmental ethics as well
3. The intensification of serious study of and engagement with canonical Jewish texts and a conscious expansion of what constitutes canonical texts
4. A full embrace of the unique possibilities and challenges of Jewish life in a sovereign democratic Jewish state

These four phenomena are simultaneously changing the character of liberal Judaism. Theologically, they have drastically expanded the possible contexts and ways in which liberal Jews, as well as all Jews, can live a religious life by increasing the possibilities for locating God's presence and hearing God's commanding voice. These new theological possibilities will allow for and even necessitate broader horizons of theological activity for the current and following generations.

"Standing on the Shoulders of Giants"

These broader horizons are possible not only because of the new context but also as a direct result of decades of study and application of the insights of the theologians before us whose modern and postmodern liberal thought made for vibrant liberal Jewish spiritual communities, seminaries, and *batei midrash* (houses of study) and thus the possibility of this next stage of Jewish thought. In naming seven categories, which can now serve as the centerpieces of the next stage of liberal Jewish thought, I certainly stand "on the shoulders of giants,"[6] benefiting from the insights of generations of Jewish scholars and thinkers that have proceeded me, especially those of four of my teachers in particular, including two liberal theologians, Eugene B. Borowitz and Rachel Adler, and two Orthodox theologians, David Hartman and Irving (Yitz) Greenberg. For more than two decades I have studied the writings of—and sat at the feet of—Borowitz, Greenberg, and Hartman, learning also from their leadership and personal examples. One of the central ideas they raise as theologians responding to the encounter of Judaism with modernity and postmodernity is a renewed focus on the possibilities of covenant as a central theological framework. If properly interpreted in the contemporary reality, covenant can, in a variety of modalities explicated differently by each thinker, continue to serve as the underpinning of much Jewish commitment. These three thinkers, together with Rachel Adler, whose *Engendering Judaism* opens new frontiers for Jewish theology and ritual, also share the capacity to employ additional strategies in order to address the modern crisis of faith and commitment (and which ensures that their theologies are relevant to the Jewish community at large and not to a single stream or community). To be sure, the next phase of liberal Jewish theology and the following seven categories are possible because of their works.

New Categories and New Questions—"Renew the Old and Sanctify the New"[7]

Given these new possibilities for Jewish commitment and the increase in possible entrances to holiness and achieving closeness to God through these four new areas of Jewish liberal intensive engagement, a different set—or perhaps a different configuration—of liberal religious categories is also necessary. Some of these categories I propose for the next stage are ancient, some are redefined, and others are newly integrated given the experience of liberal Jewish life in the sovereign Jewish State of Israel.

I believe that the next stage of Jewish theology will need to include the following seven categories of religious faith and behavior:

1. An expanded notion of the covenantal relationship with God in which a liberal Jew sees him- or herself as very much "claimed" or commanded by God (expressed through regular prayer and observance of other rituals) while still autonomously choosing to engage in the encounter with tradition that then leads to the sense of being claimed[8]

2. A wider liberal community engaged in the intensive study of canonical Jewish texts and their interpretations leading to the creation of new liberal religious commentaries

3. A deepening sense of obligation to and involvement in the Jewish People as a whole, including the Jewish People in the Jewish State, as well as less ambivalent commitments to the welfare of non-Jews as well[9]

4. Social, political, and religious commitment to upholding the human dignity of all human beings in all countries, which includes equality for women in all aspects of religious and political life and an essential ethical concern for all "others"

5. Continued insistence on radical freedom expressed in covenantaly limited autonomy for the individual with regard to religious observance because of our understanding of the modern self and the necessity of conscience for morality

6. An assertion of the centrality of the Land of Israel and the religious, ethical, and political significance of the State of Israel

7. Increasing liturgical and ritual creativity responding to the spiritual and physical experiences and needs of both women and men

In order to further clarify the contours of this relatively new situation, I will expand on three of these categories of faith and explain how they find expression in my religious life and the kind of new questions that they pose for the next stage of liberal Jewish theology.

Of Rapture and Rupture: On God with Whom I Live in Covenant

Often I think we are dangling in the air, grasping for a new way to cross the abyss between our human existence and a real, meaningful relationship with God and with Jewish tradition. The Chasidic master Pinchas of Koretz (1726–1791), a student of the Baal Shem Tov, taught that ultimately a person cannot attain closeness with God by watching another person. Specifically, a person cannot rely on modeling his or her behavior in prayer based on the behavior of others in order to attempt to cross the abyss that exists between the human being and God, but rather that this journey across the abyss is inherently an individual one, based ultimately on the experiences of a single soul. He compared such attempts to walking on a tightrope, which if you tried to learn to do it by watching another and attempted to move your feet and balance yourself the same way, you would surely fall into the abyss every time. The only way to cross the abyss is to attempt it and find your own way, your own balance, your own movements. This approach toward prayer inherently diminishes the capacity of any single stance to be one that will allow for the spirituality of all people. It necessitates a great plurality of spiritual possibilities.

Blessed Is the One Who Created Me a Woman

Studying Chasidic texts about the movement of the male body in prayer, however, led me one more step away from considering, as much of Jewish text does, the male Jewish physical reality as the definition or standard for Jewish prayer, much less for Jewish existence. In fact, studying the spiritual phenomenology of the male body further developed my awareness of the extent to which the physicality of my body is a core feature of my religious experience, not in a social/cultural sense in which modernity teaches me it should be accommodated and accepted, but in a very deep theological sense. Created in the image of God, I was created female, a blessing different from that of being created male, and which, of course, should in no way negatively impact the ways in which

I might seek out God both as an individual and as a member of the community of Israel. While one might think that rational egalitarian Judaism best achieves that assurance of access to God regardless of gender, in fact, my experiences of marriage, pregnancy, childbirth, nursing, and mothering have appropriately turned this classic liberal view on its head. Rather than becoming irrelevant theologically, my gender has become precisely and decidedly more relevant in how I experience God's presence in the world and how I understand myself to be claimed by God. Literally containing, sustaining, and painfully but joyfully giving birth to new life changed much of how I approach the question of the role of the body and gender in fulfilling God's goals for the Jewish People on both collective and individual levels. Giving birth to Israeli children was not only about personal or familial fulfillment, but also about fulfilling a greater sense of what my fully gendered existence should and could mean for the Jewish People, beyond the essentialism of being a woman, as well as beyond the ideology of being equal. Being a Jewish mother has a much larger meaning than a simple liberal stance of not relinquishing any possible religious activities because I am a woman, but rather has meant a double emphasis on the necessity to respond to God's reality by going far beyond myself to take ultimate responsibility for others, and to literally give birth to and shape the possibility of Judaism in the future. My gender, my body, and the specific physical experiences of being a mother to new and fragile life, to Jewish children in a Jewish State, all have a radical impact on the ways in which I experience God and Jewish peoplehood, and how I dream about the future of Israel and of Judaism. In some inexplicable way, deeply related to my sense of awe, wonder, and gratitude, my love for my children has only intensified my love of God, my love of the Jewish People, and my love of the Land and of all God's creations. It has made me simultaneously more religiously particularistic, universalistic, feminist, and Zionist. In other words, the more mainstream liberal, yet increasingly postmodern Judaism I might have articulated a couple of decades ago has been transformed not only by my intensified learning and observance, by also by my gender and my life in Israel.

Encountering God in Torah Study and Jewish Law

I don't think I ever doubted the existence of a real, authoritative, and demanding God. From what I learned and experienced in Jewish prayer and study, and in the context of communal life, my sense of God's commanding presence has been astonishingly constant. However, I do not always know how to find God in the context of personal and collective struggles, how to pray to God, how to understand the impenetrable commandments of Torah, much less the later rabbinic interpretations of them, and what to do with the deep ethical conflicts that sometimes emerge given my/our modern and absolute commitment to the human dignity inherent in a culture that is built on an interpretative tradition.[10] To be sure, some communities of Jews seem to love Torah more than God, some God more than Torah, and some both God and Torah more than the collectivity of the Jewish People, much less the people of Israel, or the State of Israel. (And some love the secular reality of the State as though it were a god.) Yet I cannot imagine a Jewish theology without all of them, much less a Jewish future without the reality of each fully embraced.

Indeed, much of liberal theology until recent decades emphasized the God of ethical monotheism clarified by Hermann Cohen as well as the notion that God did not literally give Torah to Moses or to the Jewish People on Sinai.[11] Rather, Torah is the product of the minds and hands of human beings, perhaps divinely inspired, over the generations, an accounting of the Jewish People's encounters with God and their best understanding of what God demands of them.[12] Given the human role in revelation, ongoing or not, human beings' continued interpretation of sacred texts are just that, human interpretations meant to evolve and change over time, responding to the needs of the Jewish People in their changing specific historical situations. We might ask, how can Halakhah *not* change given how different so many realities are today? The reality of who women, homosexuals, slaves, the blind, the deaf, and non-Jews are today vis-à-vis the larger Jewish community (as opposed to who they were and how they were perceived in ancient and medieval times) necessitates changes in Jewish law. That Jewish law changes seems necessary, yet *how* it changes and who has the authority to change it are areas where different streams of Judaism have and will likely continue to disagree. This is a reality that I see as part of the blessing of the pluralism of modern Jewish life and necessary for its healthy evolution. Human involvement and interpretation do not threaten God's authority, but rather establish it. My sense of God both existentially and textually is that God demands and even enjoys the role of human interpretation, and that is why God is portrayed as laughing the laugh of the proud parent when a talmudic debate between Rabbis becomes extreme.[13]

But while God might demand human involvement in the interpretation of Jewish law, does God really need my involvement? Or the involvement of women at all? The more I sought out places of intense engagement with the process of interpreting Judaism's sacred texts, the more I found places where women were and have remained absent or minimally present. There have been a few powerful exceptions to this observation, and I have clung to them and to the more fully human and fully Jewish expressions that emerge from them. The experience of studying Torah and its endless rabbinic interpretations as an experience of "rejoicing in the richness and complexity of the divine word, and, by implication, of the divine reality"[14] is descriptive of what happens in more and more places and has led to greater spiritual needs among liberal Jews than what the institutions in place could initially respond to.

The methodology of places like the Shalom Hartman Institute, which has been my intellectual and professional home for most of the last decade, involves studying layers of traditional text with all the rigor of an intensive *beit midrash* combined with the best methods of inquiry. This approach has proven the value of Torah study for the development of theology. The study of canonical texts must continue to be the ground from which all Jewish ideas spring. It is that foundation that will continue to sustain and inspire us both intellectually and spiritually, as individuals and as the Jewish People in unimaginable ways.

For liberal Jews, this kind of experience confirms that we need not avoid getting passionately involved with the text, rather that the richness of our religious lives depends on it. Now we can and must be more source-based in our learning and living, which simultaneously connects us to the voices of our tradition, to other Jews who base their religious lives on such texts, and to the language of the State of Israel.

Two important questions already emerge from this discussion of these categories: Might the next phase of liberal Jewish theology include the possibility of the members of some communities choosing autonomously to collectively be halakhically observant? And, given a generation-long intensified commitment to the study of sacred texts, yet the rejection of the relevance of legal codes, might liberal scholars organically begin to create a new kind of sacred literature, non-legal in character, in which interpretations of text and the implications for behavior are collected and are treated as newly created but nonetheless sanctified texts?

The Renewed Religious Possibilities of the Land of Israel, Modern Israel

These commitments to spirituality and intellectual rigor taken together with the religious commitment to more effectively take care of God's creatures and God's earth as universal values, as well as the people and the Land of Israel in particular, change the types of liberal Jewish communities that are needed. Yet, at the same time, a renewed effort to engage with Israel for the sake of better understanding one's Jewish identity characterizes more of the liberal approach to Israel and thus the kind of partners that now exist throughout the Diaspora. This category of religious commitment to Israel is too new to fully appreciate its theological consequences. I made *aliyah* not just out of love of the Jewish People and a sense of the unique historic privilege of being able to choose to make my home in and to contribute to an independent democratic Jewish State, but also out of a commitment to the significance of and a love of the *land* of Israel. While it seems unlikely from my postmodern liberal training, I also often have the ongoing sense that I have greater closeness with God here in Israel and that our greater historical, social, and spiritual responsibilities here result in a closer relationship. So living in Israel is very much a religious as well as a political act.

Indeed, this privilege of living in Israel also comes with heavy undeniable responsibilities: to ensure that this phenomenal experiment of Jewish nationalism, the return and rebirth of the Jewish People, is a source of blessing in the world. Yes, loving this People in this Land at this time requires me to take political stands because of my religious choices. I am responsible for how the government of the State of Israel treats its minorities as well as the populations in the territories. That is the difficult spiritual price for the religious freedom to seek out God in the Land of Israel and to create a homeland for the Jewish People. But from Martin Buber I learn that this is a necessity and not an impossible task. It too raises new questions for the next phase of Jewish theology in which Israel becomes a much more significant category.

Toward a New Liberal Theology

Being both radically free and radically claimed in the next phase will become less of a tension and more of an opportunity. Now that several generations of Reform Jews have fully understood what it means to have autonomy, perhaps the next several will come to understand what it means to be claimed, to feel that being in a covenantal relationship with God entails a set of behaviors that previous codifiers of Jewish law could not have foreseen, yet which anchor the lives of future generations in Jewish practice, both as particular Jewish selves, as Borowitz teaches us, and as citizens of the world with continued responsibility toward others. Indeed, as Abraham Joshua Heschel taught us, "the mountain of history is hanging over our heads."[15] We must choose to renew our covenant with God, both for the sake of our own spiritual lives and for the sake of the ethical existence of all of God's creatures.

Can Traditional Jewish Theology Still Speak to (Some of) Us?

MARC B. SHAPIRO, PHD

I DON'T OFTEN GIVE MUCH thought to God, and in this I don't think that I am unusual in my community. Much like a young child takes his parents' existence for granted, so too many Orthodox Jews, myself included, generally relate to God in this fashion. Instead of pondering the Almighty, we focus on the myriad rituals we believe bring us closer to God.

The Kotzker Rebbe famously attacked the *mitnagdim* (opponents to Chasidic Judaism) as being in awe of the *Shulchan Arukh* rather than of God, and Abraham Joshua Heschel supposedly revised the jibe so that it focused on Orthodox Jews as a whole. While there is more than a kernel of truth in this comment, it is also the case that for many in the Orthodox world, the most exalted religious meaning is found in observance of Jewish law and traditions, not in pondering theological mysteries. While outsiders are usually mystified by our attention to Halakhah, for us life is unimaginable without it. We lovingly perform the various commandments with the confidence that we are carrying out the will of God as it

---

Marc B. Shapiro, PhD, is the Weinberg Chair of Judaic Studies at the University of Scranton. He is author of *Between the Yeshiva World and Modern Orthodoxy* and *The Limits of Orthodox Theology*, both of which were National Jewish Book Award finalists.

was revealed so long ago. Since, as Job was made aware, any attempt to understand God is doomed to failure, the best we can do is attach ourselves to God, and the way to do this is through the commandments. For me, and many like me, that is enough.

It is true that Jewish philosophers have speculated at length about God, what God is (or what God is not). Many of these philosophers even felt that they could prove God's existence. Yet proving the existence of a deity, even a creator, is so far removed from a Jewish belief in God, the God of our forefathers (and foremothers), that from a religious perspective it is largely an exercise in futility. For Judaism is not about belief in "a" god, but in the God who revealed the divine presence to our ancestors and prophets, and this is certainly not something that can be proven.

Yet even though there is nothing in the way of absolute proof for the God of Israel, that doesn't mean that there aren't hints, or signs, of God's presence. Most of these are of the private sort, when a believer senses the presence of the Divine in his or her midst. Yet the greatest sign, and the one that is most meaningful to me, is the history of the Jewish People. The miraculous story of the survival of Judaism and the Jews is the greatest example of providence known to humankind. While a person can argue about how much, if anything, that happens in a person's life is due to God's providence, it is hard not to see God's hand in the ups and downs of our people throughout the generations. This is where God's presence has always been the most tangible for me.

Of course, different people have different perspectives, and this leads to the question of the limits of Jewish belief, and what can be deemed an authentic or coherent Jewish theology. The response many would give is the utilitarian perspective; that is, a belief system that assists in Jewish continuity and gives people meaning in their lives is authentic. Yet for me, matters are more complicated, for while the above definition will please many, it leaves out any consideration of traditional Jewish beliefs.

I do not think that an authentic Jewish theology can entirely remove God from the world and deny the existence of a revelation to humanity. How God relates to the world, and what one means by revelation, will obviously be disputed, and have been throughout history. Yet I don't think it is possible to begin to speak about Jewish theology without an acceptance of God's presence in the world and God's inspiration (however defined) of certain people who were able to achieve a closeness with the Divine.

I say this even though I personally am comfortable removing God from almost everything that takes place in the world, a position that many in my own community will view as inauthentic. While my view is certainly a break from what is often expressed among the Orthodox, Maimonides, the preeminent medieval Jewish philosopher, and other thinkers of his time believed that the world generally functions according to the laws of nature and humans act in an autonomous fashion. They did not assume that religiosity meant seeing God's hand in everyday events or that God was continually pulling the strings of this world.

I have found this naturalistic perspective to be religiously helpful in many ways, not least of which religion no longer focuses on what God does for me but how best I should live my life. With such an approach, theodicy, among other things, is no longer the burning problem it usually is for believers. Needless to say, such a perspective means that the liturgy of the High Holy Days, which speaks of God's involvement in all that happens, is not to be read literally.

I am often happy that I no longer serve in a rabbinic role since while my theology certainly has a proud lineage, it is probably not the sort of approach that would work well in a communal setting. When a family is grieving over some tragic loss, they want to be told—and to believe—that their loss is part of some higher purpose and that it fits into some larger plan. Being told that bad things happen to good people because, well, sometimes bad things just happen to good people, will probably not be much comfort. This is especially true in the Orthodox world, which in recent years has seen a number of leading rabbis who are able to explain not only why the little things go wrong (it must be that women are not dressed modestly enough), but even why God chooses to send a tsunami.

So much of Jewish theology focuses on the particulars, on how God and the Jews relate to each other. What is the role of the non-Jew in all this? Here I find myself at odds with much of current theological thinking. The "in" position is to assert that all theologies are equal and that we should celebrate the diverse religions of the world. Such a celebration of the diversity of God's world is more than tolerance and even more than pluralism; it is recognition of the truth found in all religions. This approach has also influenced some Jewish theologians to speak of multiple sacred covenants. For awhile now, many Jews have been very keen to have the Vatican declare that God's covenant with the Jews is still in force. Believing this was achieved, certain Jewish theologians decided to return the favor from the Jewish perspective, the exact sort of quid pro quo theology that the late Rabbi Joseph B. Soloveitchik was so concerned about.

My own perspective is that while it is true that no one religion can encompass all of God's truth, a person should not conclude that there is no falsehood in the area of religion. While an authentic Jewish theology need not deny that other groups and nations also have their own special relationship with God, I regard it as a betrayal of historic Jewish theology for Jews to hedge on the issue of Jesus's divinity or the authenticity of Muhammad's revelation.

How then is one to evaluate other theological systems? My answer is that if they help people to lead good lives, lives that center around helping others and being good citizens, then they are valuable religions. There is absolutely no contradiction between validating the integrity and value of another theological system while at the same time denying the theological truth claims asserted by this religion. An outsider to a faith only needs to look at the result of the religion, namely, does it make good people? The details of the particular religion's theology should be left to those in the fold. Following the wise philosophical principle of what's good for the goose is good for the gander, I have never been able to understand why some Jews get so exercised about whether other religions grant Judaism a sufficient amount of theological significance.

Just as I don't believe that the postmodern turn has required the adoption of a new theology, I don't think that the new atheism offers a significant challenge. We can now, much more than in the past, appreciate how significant our surroundings are in influencing how we formulate concepts, including concepts of religion. Yet this does not mean that the door has been opened to religious relativism. By the same token, the recent atheist writers have been able to call attention to a good deal of foolishness and evil in religion, yet this does not disqualify all of religion.

There have been sophisticated atheist tracts for many years now, and the new writers cannot add much in the way of philosophical perspectives to what has already been stated. As for the foolishness and evils of religion that they identify, while recent years have seen new examples of each, the new atheists are pushing a caricature of religion. Since, at the end of the day, no one is going to be able to prove or disprove the existence of God, when it comes to judging the value of religion we have to look at the adherents. From such an examination, the believers as a whole come out looking very good, especially in terms of their commitments to helping the less fortunate and making the world a better place. This alone should entitle religion to a better hearing than it is currently receiving at the hands of certain writers.

Finally, let me turn to the State of Israel, the creation of which is the most momentous occurrence in the last two thousand years of Jewish life. Has it had an impact on Jewish theology? Without a doubt. How could it not have? The creation and sustenance of the State of Israel, against such great odds, is one of the most tangible signs of the existence of God and God's covenant with Jewry.

One must be careful that the creation of the State, and Jewish self-rule, not lead to radical changes in theology. Unfortunately, for a number of years now I have been concerned about the development of a radical theology in Israel that does not seem to be a passing fad. A vision of God concerned with the Jewish People to the almost complete exclusion of all others, a vengeful God whose people must always be ready to strike at God's enemies, a God who has begun a redemptive process and insists that we believe that history as we know it is near its end—all these ideas can be found at the heart of messianic religious Zionism.

With such an outlook, no territorial compromises can be considered, and all that is necessary for a secure State is unwavering faith in the Rock of Israel. This theology, which removes all need for Realpolitik in dealing with the security and demographic problems Israel faces, and instead places everything in God's hand, is an example of the dangers of a new theology engendered by the reborn State of Israel.

A QUEST
FOR GOD

A Quest-Driven Faith

RABBI ELLIOT J. COSGROVE, PHD

FAITH BEGINS WITH ME, not God.

A person of faith is designated as such not because she or he is in possession of a Truth, the nature of which another person cannot access. Rather a person of faith has made the willed choice to seek to understand and stand in relation to the mystery of our existence. Such a faith recognizes that while the object of any declaration of faith may be God, the subject of those same statements is a humanity profoundly limited in its theological vision. Theology must be framed humbly and tentatively, ever mindful of twentieth-century Christian theologian Karl Barth's comment "The angels will laugh when they read my theology." An aspirational vocation, faith can best be described as an ongoing quest to know an ever-elusive God.

A non-fundamentalist theologian readily admits that a complete understanding of God is forever beyond human comprehension. From Moses being informed that "man may not see Me and live" (Exodus 33:20), our attempts to grasp the nature of the Divine reveal the asymptotic

---

Rabbi Elliot J. Cosgrove, PhD, is rabbi at Park Avenue Synagogue in Manhattan. He did undergraduate work at the University of Michigan in English and Middle Eastern studies, received his Master of Hebrew Letters from American Jewish University, studied at the Schechter Institute of Judaic Studies in Jerusalem, and was ordained at The Jewish Theological Seminary. His doctorate from the University of Chicago Divinity School is in the history of Judaism.

nature of the theological project. This admission, however, need not be understood as a concession. Quite the contrary, doubt may be the most sincere (and incontrovertible) religious sentiment we have at our disposal. It is the deep humility wrought by an abiding awareness of our inability to describe God fully that is perhaps the only place to begin a theological conversation of integrity.

It is these two interrelated claims, the bottom-up nature of theology and the unknowability of God, that constitute the starting point for my faith as a Jew. Such a faith does not seek to define God, but rather encompasses a lifetime of approximations and affirmations, collectively reflecting a desire to draw close to my creator. Like love, faith does not demand a total knowledge of the other for that relationship to be significant, even all-encompassing. As with the dialogue between lovers in the Song of Songs, a covenantal relationship is not contingent on its consummation. Always seeking but never found, always thirsting but never quenched, it is our passionate search for our espoused Partner that is the point and power of our quest for God.[1]

In a quest-driven faith, Jewish prayer, inquiry, and observance become a series of opportunities for discovery: of the self, others, and God. Every act of prayer signals not merely the affirmation of hoary catechisms but an effort toward constructing a relationship with the historic God of the Jewish People and all of humanity. So too, by searching the texts of our tradition, I seek to retrieve Judaism's spiritual treasures to give voice to my spiritual questions. Torah is not something to be accepted or rejected, rather it is a palimpsest, to be searched and probed in order to discover again and again traces of God's voice. Finally, by performing *mitzvot*, I reach out toward my God in heaven and the divine spark embedded in all of humanity. In a quest-driven faith, *mitzvot* stop becoming a list of do's and don'ts, and start becoming a series of opportunities to bind myself to God's will.

The power of Torah, prayer, and observance is not dependent on determining what does or does not reflect the divine will. Rather it is by way of devotional prayer, study, and *mitzvot* that I am provided with the tools to address the spiritual yearnings lodged in my soul. My faith, expressed in these idioms, collectively reflect my willed longing to search for God.

People may differ as to whether or not such a quest-driven theology represents a new sort of faith. It is undoubtedly a sign of the times when the trajectory of the religious experience is not God to humanity, but the other way round—the sovereign self leading to God. Certainly such a posture makes explicit the self-constructed nature of belief. The challenge of atheism is not terribly interesting inasmuch as I readily grant the volitional dimension to my faith. Faced with the awe of creation, the wonders of existence, and the mysteries lurking in my soul, I consciously *choose* to find the vocabulary, rituals, and spiritual demeanor that serve as the spiritual scaffolding to my existence. I opt to actively ponder the imponderable. The atheist is rightfully weary of the evils inflicted in the name of those claiming certitude vis-à-vis God's will, and I do not begrudge his skepticism of religious language altogether. In Jamesian terms (William James 1842–1910), I have made a willed choice to back "the religious hypothesis" just as the atheist has chosen not to do so. Who is right? I have no idea. As long as we agree to respect the integrity of our respective choices, I see no upside to prolonging this dispute.

But in such a schema, can we make any positive statements about the nature of God? Once we have dispensed with all our qualifications, dare we speak of God? Or does the mere utterance of descriptive terms impose a lexicon upon that which transcends the capacity of human discourse? Certainly as Jews, God makes certain claims on our being, both as members of a covenanted people and a common humanity: a historic concern with the Jewish People, an ongoing involvement and presence in the affairs of humanity, a set of expectations for human behavior with a concomitant language of reward and punishment, a belief in the afterlife, revelation, to name but a few. Do we believe in any of this? Whether defined as dogmas or a sacred cluster of ideals, the "God-Idea" and its manifold implications has always been an integral part of Judaism. Faced with the uncomfortable options of saying too much or too little about God, what dare we say?

I believe that a quest represents a third-way approach to this age-old dilemma. A quest signals an interpretive mode whereby the autonomous self stands in dialogue with the received texts of our tradition, all in an effort to respond to the questions of the age. My notions of God result from engagement with Jewish literature and the Jewish community of the past, present, and future. Time and again, biblical and rabbinic literature has proven to be sufficiently limber to allow me to wrestle with the questions knocking at my being. The God I believe in is not monolithic, nor is the God of biblical and rabbinic literature, and for this I am grateful. My arguments for observance, belief in the afterlife, and notions of revelation are ever-evolving but have until this time been able to find a home in an interpretively elastic and pluralistic textual tradition. Similarly, in Jewish prayer and practice, I continue to find the verbal and non-verbal means to express the outpouring of my heart and obligations before God and humanity. In times of joy and pain, solitude and community, my ventures into the storehouse of Jewish literature and practice provide me with the tools by which to approach what is ultimately an ever-elusive Truth. As a Jewish educator, it is my task to represent the richness of our tradition to other Jews on their own quests, providing them with the confidence to embark on their own journeys. Finally, as a Jew, I consider myself a participant in this ever-growing corpus of Jewish response to an ineffable God. Whether our modest contributions prove to be heretical, essential, or irrelevant to a future Jewish canon, only time will tell. Questions of authenticity can never be answered in our own lifetimes, and even then, arguments are bound to persist. The great strength of a quest-driven faith is that it permits me to affirm my own beliefs, even as they develop, all the while respecting the integrity of another person's path.

Yet, in articulating the pillars of my own faith, the central challenge to Jewish theology today also stands revealed. The challenge to Jewish theology is not from atheists, biblical criticism, inexplicable evil, or any new epistemological challenge. I believe American Jews are altogether religious inasmuch as we employ William James's definition of religion as the "the feelings, acts, and experiences of individual men in their solitude, so far as they apprehend themselves to stand in relation to whatever they may consider the Divine."[2] Our challenge is not theological but sociological. It is the "Jewish" of Jewish theology that is facing a threat. My theology, though probably far too liberal in its orientation for my more traditional co-religionists, can at least be loosely defined as Jewish because of my insistence to conduct my religious quest in dialogue with Judaism. My decision to express my faith by way of a Jewish toolbox arrives by way of a series of a priori claims on my identity—in my case, born into a traditional Jewish family. I may learn about and even admire the paths by which a diverse humanity aspires toward the Divine, but it has never been a live option for me to join another faith community. As long as I choose to lead a life of faith, it will be a Jewish one; my sympathies with my people are simply too anchored to have it otherwise.

I fear that fewer and fewer Jews are willing to express their faith in such partisan terms. In other words, Jews are increasingly disinclined to explore their faith in dialogue with their Judaism. In an era of the sovereign self, waning Jewish literacy, and a diminishing tug of the internal and eternal bonds of peoplehood, the decision to seek answers within Jewish literature and practice is a decision that fewer Jews are taking. The task of our generation is not to convince people to be religious minded. Our charge is to cultivate communities filled with individuals impelled to turn to their Judaism to express their faith. What is needed is a narrative and communal structure capable of laying claim to and educating an alienated Jew. Jewish theology and Jewish peoplehood are entirely interdependent. Without theology, Jewish peoplehood becomes an arbitrary series of folkways. Without a sense of peoplehood, Jewish theology becomes a road untraveled. As Reconstructionist ideologue Rabbi Mordecai Kaplan counseled, Jews must come to understand that the "self-identification of the individual Jew with [sic] the Jewish People is the source of the mystical element in the Jewish Religion."[3]

Our faith, like our lives, takes on far more meaning when we view it as a quest. The paradigm of our tradition from leaving the Garden of Eden, to Abraham's journey, to the wilderness wanderings is the notion of a pilgrimage. Faith is not about beginnings or endings, but about process, forward momentum, and opportunities for discovery. The choice to embark on an ever-active quest for God in dialogue with the riches of our tradition signals an empowered yet deeply humble choice, capable of steering between the options of secularism and fundamentalism. Not in the answers it provides, but in the spiritual posture it recommends, such a quest directed both toward heaven and the Jewish tradition holds the promise of enabling us to stand in relation to our God, to whom we owe our existence.

Theological Proximity
The Quest for Intimacy with God

SIMON COOPER, PHD

IN THIS SHORT ARTICLE I begin to map out my formulation for an ongoing theological project for thinking Jewry: the quest for intimacy with God. It is a formulation that I have derived from my reading of two of the great philosophical voices of our tradition, Maimonides and Rabbi Joseph B. Soloveitchik, and that seems to me increasingly relevant in today's religious environment. The fundamentals of the approach are as follows: (1) a person's religious life should be about developing and nurturing a personal relationship with God; (2) that this is best achieved via the type of philosophical approach favored by both Maimonides and Soloveitchik; and (3) that a knowledge of secular philosophy, and secular studies in general, is of immense importance to this ongoing quest. I will now attempt to justify this project.

In the twelfth century, Maimonides (Rabbi Moses ben Maimon) articulated his philosophy of Judaism. Spanning several decades and several landmark contributions to the canon of post-rabbinic literature, Maimonides developed a unique understanding of the religion. His unique understanding centered around the delicate interplay between

Simon Cooper, PhD, earned his doctoral degree in contemporary covenantal thought at King's College, London. He is a teaching fellow at the London School of Jewish Studies and is also editorial assistant for the *Journal of Jewish Studies*.

belief and action within the life of faith. While rabbinic Judaism had emphasized action over belief—the perfection of the performance of the *mitzvot* representing the highest goal of Jewish worship—Maimonides instead posited the need for correct beliefs to underpin those actions.

This Maimonidean approach comes across most clearly in his commentary on chapter 10 of the Mishnah in *Sanhedrin*, the section known as *Perek Cheilek*, because it deals with a person's portion (*cheilek*) in the world-to-come. The Rabbis in this section of the Oral Law are discussing deeds by which a Jewish person may lose his or her portion in the world-to-come. The assumption here is that the Rabbis understand gaining or losing your portion in the world-to-come as being dependent upon your deeds. If you keep the *mitzvot* then you will gain entry to the world-to-come, and if you perform certain grievous transgressions then you are in danger of losing your share. Maimonides adds to this rabbinic understanding by making the quite revolutionary assertion that in order to be considered for the world-to-come you had to not only *do* certain things, but also to *think* certain things.

This was perhaps the first, and most significant, attempt to bring dogma or creed into Judaism. Maimonides' famous Thirteen Principles of Faith, which appear within this commentary on *Perek Cheilek*, are enumerated in order to explain exactly what a Jew must believe in order to be considered truly part of the community, and in order to gain his or her portion in the world-to-come. What is significant is not the specific content of those beliefs, but that they are considered by Maimonides to be requirements. For the first time, we are being told what to think. Moreover, there is more than an implicit suggestion throughout Maimonides' work that if there were to be a hierarchy between practice and belief, the former would be subordinate to the latter. There is a debate within Maimonidean scholarship as to whether Maimonides considered moral and spiritual perfection possible without performance of the commandments at all, and the mere fact that such a debate exists testifies to the supremacy of belief over action in his work.

I am strongly drawn to this Maimonidean approach, despite its divergence from mainstream Orthodox Judaism today. Sadly (in my opinion), Judaism is characterized today largely in terms of action—it is what you *do* or *don't do* that defines your Jewish credentials. However the word *orthodoxy* (as opposed to *orthopraxy*) denotes belief, and the religious life should center on a person's belief system. Maimonides boldly attempted to revolutionize Judaism, and his attempt still resonates today among those people for whom Jewish life is about trying to build a personal relationship with God. Building that relationship will necessitate an investigation not only into a person's own belief system, but also into an understanding of possible conceptions of God, a subject much favored by Maimonides.

Put simply, it is impossible to attempt to come to know God when you have no understanding of what God is, and that is why Maimonides insists on believers entertaining correct notions of the Divine Entity prior to beginning worship. The thinker who best encapsulated this kind of approach in the modern era is the modern Jewish philosopher Joseph B. Soloveitchik, better known as "The Rav." Soloveitchik's work exhibits considerable tension and unease. At the crux of this unease is the inherent difficulty of living a life of faith. The true person of faith is torn asunder by his or her attempts at understanding the covenantal relationship with God. The faithful person "oscillates between ecstasy in God's companionship and despair when he feels abandoned by God"[1] and struggles to comprehend "the awesome dichotomy of God's involvement in the drama of creation, and His exaltedness above and remoteness from this very drama."[2] In other words, the precise nature of the faithful person's relationship with God perplexes and troubles him. How can God be at the same time concerned and involved in the world, and utterly above and beyond both the human realm and human understanding? A knowledge of this intractable problem leads to the existential loneliness felt by Soloveitchik's "lonely man of faith."

Soloveitchik's man of faith is intrinsically linked to a Maimonidean conception of Judaism, because the man of faith is concerned with understanding the precise nature of his relationship with

131

his creator (if, in fact, it can be classified as a relationship at all). Based on a quite novel interpretation of the first two chapters of *Bereshit* (Genesis), Soloveitchik presents two alternative human personality types, Adam the first and Adam the second; that is, the Adam created in chapter 1, and the Adam created in chapter 2. It is Adam the second who is utterly preoccupied with God, largely because of the nature of Adam the second's birth, when God breathed into his nostrils, forging a closer bond between God and Adam the second than perhaps was present in Adam the first's creation. Adam the first was created in God's image, after God's likeness. Soloveitchik's lonely man of faith, then, perhaps more closely resembles Adam the second's character type, who will always yearn to return to the proximity with God that he felt at the start of his life.

Adam the second's experience resonates with us all. There are moments in life when, if we are extremely lucky, we feel the divine presence in our lives. But these are only fleeting moments, far outweighed by the vast majority of time when we do not and cannot feel close to God. And yet it seems only right and proper to me that the essence of a person's Judaism should be about adopting a framework within which one can continue along the pursuit of this dream, namely proximity to, or closeness to, God. Maimonides writes that "it must be man's aim, after having acquired the knowledge of God, to deliver himself up to Him, and to have his heart constantly filled with longing for Him."[3] Indeed, Maimonides reinterprets the messianic era to complement this vision of the ultimate goal of worship; even in the messianic era people's enjoyment will be based on the level of their knowledge of God because, quite literally, what they will enjoy is their knowledge of God. Without that knowledge, there will be minimal scope for enjoyment.

Neither Maimonides nor Soloveitchik make explicit exactly *how* a person goes about attaining this proximity to God. Indeed, it would be quite remarkable if they had done so. Surely proximity to God is a personal vision, and attempting to attain it is therefore very much a personal quest. It is unsurprising, in this regard, that Maimonides was criticized for suggesting that man could (and at times should) remove himself from his community in order to live a secluded life, which would afford him better opportunity for the fulfillment of his task. Both Maimonides' vision for the future of religion and Soloveitchik's depiction of the lonely man of faith are personal rather than communal visions. However, the communal framework can certainly help the individual to reach his or her goal.

Ultimately, in the view of both thinkers, each and every Jewish person has to attempt to understand his or her relationship to God, rather than falling back on a kind of communal safety net. It is precisely because of the individual, personal quest that the life of faith demands that Soloveitchik feels impelled to describe the quest as lonely. How can a married man like Soloveitchik, with a wife, children, grandchildren, students, congregants, and numerous friends and colleagues, feel lonely? Because the loneliness is more existential than those interpersonal relationships suggest. It transcends the mundane, human, earthly realm (the realm that Soloveitchik's other hero-figure, "Halakhic Man," so reveres) and sees the world in more cosmic terms.

Despite the lack of practical guidance from either Maimonides or Soloveitchik, there are clearly lessons that can be learned here, and indeed I think we have a strong foundation from which to continue our Jewish theological endeavors in the twenty-first century. What is the precise nature of this strong foundation? Primarily, it is based on personal intimacy with God, on living a life of faith appropriating a form of close relationship with your creator. Second, it develops from a rigorous philosophical analysis of Judaism, which attempts to understand the very essence of the faith endeavor, and in doing so to highlight the fundamental principles of the faith.[4] And third, it is borne out of a firm belief in the benefit of (and indeed importance of) secular philosophy and secular studies. Both Maimonides and Soloveitchik were learned in (among other things) the secular philosophy of their day. For Maimonides, it was Aristotelian metaphysics. For Soloveitchik, it was the Western post-Enlightenment philosophical tradition (and in particular existentialist philosophy). Both incorporated significant elements of it into their articulations of Jewish faith.

The twentieth-century Jewish theologian Julius Guttmann has claimed that "the history of Jewish philosophy is the history of the successive absorptions of foreign ideas that were then transformed and analyzed according to specific Jewish points of view,"[5] and I would argue for the supreme importance of these successive absorptions of external influences. Some of the best articulations for a vibrant and coherent Jewish philosophy have always occurred at the intersection between Torah and philosophy. One could include thinkers such as Samson Raphael Hirsch and Abraham Joshua Heschel along with Maimonides and Soloveitchik, as figures whose works show profound erudition in Western and Greek philosophy at the same time as sublime mastery in Torah Judaism. These thinkers have created nuanced and attractive models for understanding the intricacies of Jewish faith, which have been enhanced and enriched because of their positive attitude toward secular learning. It is my belief that these two great thinkers and rabbis—Maimonides and Soloveitchik—should act as exemplars for a continuation of this kind of theological project. It will be a project that utilizes a rigorous philosophical analysis that is guided by both traditional and secular learning. The goal of the endeavor will be an attempt to give guidance on how to achieve proximity to God. I can think of no greater project with which to occupy thinking Jewry—academics, rabbis, and laypeople—in the years to come.

Longing to Hear Again

RABBI LEON A. MORRIS

FORMULATING A THEOLOGY for the twenty-first century requires far more modesty than earlier theological writings seemed to acknowledge. In the medieval period, theologians spelled out the minute details of correct belief with a confidence built around sets of proofs for the existence of God, for the reality of divine providence, and for the truth of revelation. In modernity such proofs fell victim to science and reason, and it became increasingly necessary to redefine or rethink our earlier theological ideas in light of an unbounded faith in the goodness of humanity and in universal ethics. While seemingly worlds apart, what premodern and modern theology shared was a posture of certainty, either about what God is or what God is not. In sharp contrast, our times are marked by great uncertainty. For many of us, contemporary theology is less about what we know to be true and more about religious ways of organizing and conceiving the world. If medieval and modern Jewish theology were prose, ours is a theology of poetry. In our time, "doing theology" is far more about meaning and elegance than a truth that ultimately lies beyond our capacity to understand.

With this in mind, theology in the twenty-first century can be understood as shaping religious narratives that attempt to reflect upon

Leon A. Morris is the rabbi of Temple Adas Israel in Sag Harbor, New York. He is the founding director of the Skirball Center for Adult Jewish Learning at Temple Emanu-El in Manhattan. He has contributed essays to the *Philadelphia Inquirer, Baltimore Sun, Sh'ma, Jewish Week* and *Beliefnet,* and has contributed a chapter entitled "Beyond Autonomy" in *Platforms and Prayer Books: Theological and Liturgical Perspectives on Reform Judaism.*

God's reality and our conception of the good life, while being keenly aware of all that lies beyond our full comprehension. With an admission that there are seemingly infinite ways of speaking about God, contemporary theology can be upfront about developing a theological narrative with an end goal in mind: the life that will be lived as a result of this theology.

What is such a life for our times? For liberal American Jews, the most urgent need of the hour is for Judaism to move us beyond the self and inspire us to transcend our isolated individualism. We seek to connect with the other, to form communities of shared purpose, and to feel a sense of genuine continuity with the Jewish past. Many of us hunger for a sense of commitment and obligation that is sufficiently compelling as to allow us to move beyond (but not entirely reject) our doubt and skepticism in order to give our lives a sense of deeper meaning and purpose.

As liberal Jews, the traditional claims of authority for our sacred texts are simply not persuasive if such claims are understood in their most literal sense. Our conception of God, and particularly the nature and content of revelation, invariably part ways from the most rigidly traditional perspective. While several generations ago such viewpoints constituted a radical rejection of core Jewish principles, for many of us the traditional claims (without being reinterpreted) are simply unconvincing from the outset. We know too much history and too much about biblical criticism to be able to seriously entertain the traditional claims of revelation. We see evidence of human (co-)authorship in each of our sacred texts. Commandments cannot be entirely isolated from sociology and anthropology and are thereby inevitably viewed as a human attempt to determine how to live in the presence of God. As a result of the breakdown of traditional conceptions of authority, the individual has emerged as the ultimate arbiter of determining a person's obligations. But personal autonomy has drastically eroded a sense of religious passion and devotion. It has minimized the role of religion in daily life and has weakened our ties to one another and to our inherited tradition.

This has been my religious dilemma for many years, and I sense that I am not alone. What is a liberal Jews to do if he or she seeks a vibrant, all-encompassing life of Jewish commitment and responsibility? A return to a premodern understanding of God and Torah is simply not possible. We cannot put the genie back in the bottle, and there is no desire to do so. The many gifts of modernity compensate for its challenges. However, we are painfully aware of how insufficient modernity's teachings are for shaping a passionate Jewish life. As Paul Mendes-Flohr, a leading scholar of modern Jewish thought, has stated, "We thus face a profound impasse. Modern individualism seems to be producing a way of life that is neither individually nor socially viable, yet a return to traditional forms would be to return to intolerable religious determinism and oppression. The question, then, is whether the older civic and biblical traditions have the capacity to reformulate themselves while simultaneously remaining faithful to their own deepest insights."[1]

A new theological approach is needed to help us to rethink and reclaim Jewish ideas and practice for an age such as ours. We seek a theology that allows for all the skepticism, critique, and analysis that modernity bequeathed to us while taking us a step beyond, to where the old language can speak to us again in new ways.

A vital philosophical concept that gives voice to this theological project is the notion of "second naïveté." The term, first coined by Peter Wust, a nineteenth-century Catholic thinker, but developed most fully by the twentieth-century philosopher Paul Ricoeur, is succinctly defined by Dr. Elie Holzer, a researcher at Bar-Ilan University, as "a critically mediated attitude toward the reality claims of religious faith."[2] The first naïveté was marked by the "immediacy of belief" in the traditional claims of religious life.[3] For us as Jews, this first naïveté includes notions such as God speaking at Mount Sinai, the Torah being written by God, and Moses receiving both the Written and Oral Torah. At some point, as a result of science, history, and source criticism, our original first naïveté was shattered. Ricoeur understands this process of demythologization as "the irreversible gain of truthfulness, intellectual honesty, objectivity."[4] Yet, Ricoeur's contribution is that this dissolution of the myth is not necessarily the final step. Once the myth becomes shattered, there is a way for it to be restored as "symbol." It is not a retreat back to *believing* in the original myth. To the contrary, it is a new way of *understanding* the myth.

> Does that mean that we could go back to a primitive naïveté? Not at all. In every way, something has been lost, irremediably lost: immediacy of belief. But if we can no longer live the great symbolisms of the sacred in accordance with the original belief in them, we can, we modern men, aim at a second naïveté in and through criticism. In short, it is by *interpreting* that we can *hear* again.[5]

Interpretation, what philosophy calls hermeneutics, is for Ricoeur the means through which the old myths and rituals can be revived. The indispensability of interpretation for Ricoeur finds its parallel in a rabbinic worldview that understood the text and its interpretation as dual products of revelation. "Even what a sharp pupil will expound before his teacher has already been given to Moses at Sinai" (JT *Pe'ah* 2:4).

A second naïveté anchored in the act of interpretation argues for the renewed centrality of *beit hamidrash* (the study hall) Jewish institutional life. Its culture engenders the kind of questioning, debate, and dialectic that mirrors the stage of critique and demythologization that causes the first naïveté to be shattered. In moving beyond critique and questioning, however, *beit hamidrash* becomes a kind of institutional embodiment of second naïveté. In the study of texts in *beit hamidrash* previous readings are often superseded by new interpretations. Again and again, old ideas are reclaimed and ancient myths are revived through the active interpretative engagement. It is *beit hamidrash* that generates, and is generated by, the kind of interpretive process that makes the revival of myth and meaning possible.

Beit hamidrash is also a model for the creative exchange and interplay between the self and the other. *Beit hamidrash* points to the way in which the interpretive life can only be lived in community. If hermeneutics makes possible the reviving of myth, then the community is an indispensable feature of a second naïveté. For example, German philosopher Georg Gadamer says "the task of hermeneutics is to clarify this miracle of understanding, which is not a mysterious communion of souls, but sharing in a common meaning."[6] Only through conversation with the other are we really able to begin to exhaust the possibility of understanding a text or experience. Seated across the table from another person, meaning and understanding emerge from the trialogue between the study partners and the text. If personal autonomy could be compared to a solitary individual sitting quietly in their library study carrel, then the model of *beit hamidrash*, with its hubbub and argument, serves as a corrective to an autonomy that is isolated and alienating.[7] In this way, *beit hamidrash* serves to remind us that autonomy is only the starting place, the unarguable fact that each person has the authority to determine the law for him- or herself. But as *beit hamidrash* makes room for community, a sense of commandedness emerges, and the classic dichotomy between autonomy and heteronomy begins to break down. Who I am is deeply affected by those with whom I engage. The experience of study allows me to bring all of who I am to the table. I am free to critique the text and apply all of my own outside knowledge to bear. But in the act of studying a text with another person in an attempt to understand it and give it meaning, a revival of this text has simultaneously occurred, and a community emerges with a shared life of symbols and common language.

Philosopher Ernst Simon "translated" Wust's notion of second naïveté into a Jewish context and additionally conceived of it being the climax of three distinct stages of human-religious development: first naivete, followed by reflective critique, followed ultimately by second naivete.[8] While Simon's stages refer to the development of an individual, let us extend his notion and apply these stages to the Jewish People collectively. When thinking chronologically about the passage from the premodern to our day, these stages take on new meaning. There are few contemporary liberal Jews who have personally experienced a first naïveté.[9] Most of us entered Jewish life long after a widespread demythologization had already occurred. First naïveté speaks of the theological landscape prior to modernity. Beginning with seventeenth-century rationalist Baruch Spinoza, but culminating in the Enlightenment, the foundational myths of Judaism were challenged and shattered by modernity. Modernity was defined, in many ways, by the second stage of criticism and reflection. However, since that time, liberal Judaism has been unable to move beyond that second stage. The contemporary liberal Jew has yet to achieve a "newfound positive orientation [that] allows him or her to resist the total claim of critical thinking, to go beyond the conclusions of his [or her] rational self and explore new realms of meaning."[10] Our embrace of critique has not yet been fully applied to the act of critique itself, as second naivete calls us to do. For some time, we have been in the final moments of that intermediary stage, standing at the precipice but not yet having crossed the threshold to a second naïveté. To be sure, we have asserted that old rituals can have meaning for us in our contemporary lives. But our goal has not been as ambitious as a full-scale revival and reclamation. To the contrary, there remains today within Reform Judaism a great deal of ambivalence toward traditional practice, grounded in the assumption that a critical approach would render such actions unnecessary at best, and superstitious at worst.

To borrow two additional terms from Ricoeur, Reform Judaism in America has for more than a century exclusively asserted a "hermeneutic of suspicion" without supplementing it with a "hermeneutic of affirmation." The latter suggests that we examine our texts and rituals in ways that would encourage their rejuvenation. Historical and critical perspectives would not be used to reject, but would serve as the background from which we would be engaged in a heartfelt attempt to embrace. This would mark a decisive shift in the orientation of liberal Judaism. For more than a century and a half, liberal Jews have routinely rejected countless practices on the basis of a sound intellectual defense ("this ritual still bears the traces of its superstitious origin"; "that commandment reflects taboos common in the ancient Near East"). A Jewish second naïveté will invite us to return to normative Jewish life in ways that do not ask us to abandon our scholarship or historicism, or suppress our ability to critique, but rather encourage us to move beyond them, to discover in the old texts and rituals new possibilities for meaning, community, and divine connection.

Before being introduced to the notion of second naïveté I found that my own religious life bore out this concept, and I suspect this is true for many of my friends and colleagues. The acceptance of biblical source criticism does not preclude me from experiencing the weightiness of a commandment in the Torah. Knowing the history of the development of *Kaddish* and the relatively late emergence of the practice of reciting it for eleven months for a deceased parent does not eliminate feeling as though my late father's soul is dependent upon my voice in order to rise to heaven. A Jewish second naivete allows for a vital merging of poetry and symbolism with responsibility and obligation. In acquiring a second naïveté, twenty-first century liberal Jews can shape a religious way of life once again anchored by classic theological constructs such as *Torah mi'Sinai* (Torah from Sinai), *b'rit* (covenant), *mitzvah* (commandment), and Halakhah (Jewish law). In reclaiming this language, our approach will be decidedly more oriented toward embrace rather than rejection, more centered around the community than the self, and more open to learning than to critique.

There is a well-known talmudic *aggadah* that stems from an overly literal understanding of the description of the children of Israel encamped at Mount Sinai awaiting revelation in Exodus 19:17, "And they took their places at the foot of the mountain."

> Rav Abdimi bar Hama bar Hasa said: This teaches that the Holy One of Blessing held the mountain over them like a bell jar and said: If you accept the Torah, fine. If not, this will be your grave. Rav Aha bar Jacob said: Nevertheless, they accepted it in the time of Ahasuerus, for it is written (Esther 9:27), "The Jews fulfilled and accepted." That is, they fulfilled what they had already accepted.
>
> (BT *Shabbat* 88a)

This *aggadah* is vital to our discussion. The book of Esther's understanding of God (and perhaps the understanding of the generation about whom it was written) stands in sharp contrast to most of the Hebrew Bible. God is hidden in the book of Esther, and the sort of obvious salvific miracles that characterize the Bible seem to be absent. What could it mean then for the people of Mordecai and Esther's generation to have *fulfilled* the Torah? And how is such a fulfillment different from *acceptance*? Perhaps theirs was a kind of second naïveté, an assertion that the Torah could indeed be fulfilled in very different times and circumstances when acceptance is far more challenging.

And for us as well, it is obvious that the power of a coercive acceptance is long gone. The Rabbis no longer have constitutive authority. The sacred nature of our central texts is conceived of in radically different ways. Our conception of the relationship between God and humanity has shifted away from pure heteronomy. From this reality, a new way must emerge that enables us to re-embrace Torah and *mitzvot*. Our urgency comes precisely because we no longer experience the mountain being suspended above our heads and yet, like the generation of Esther and Mordecai, we long for a real and lasting connection to the generation that stood at Sinai.

Walking the Walk

Rabbi Daniel Nevins

MY THEOLOGICAL PARADOX: a God whom I can describe is not worthy of my worship. This is axiomatic. God as an object is always god as an idol. How could mere creatures comprehend and describe the author of creation? Human consciousness is bound by the constraints of our limited experience and imagination. What are a few decades of education in the context of eternity? What perspective can ever be gained—even by the boldest of explorers—of the vastness of space? Our knowledge is pathetically limited, and yet we presume to speak of the eternal One. The morning prayer of the Jewish liturgy has it right—*Mah anachnu, mah chayeinu, mah chasdeinu, mah tzidkeinu, mah g'vurateinu?* "What are we in comparison to God? What are our lives, our morality, our strength?" Even the wisest and most righteous people die and are forgotten. "What is a person ... that You should know [or be known to] him?" (Psalm 144:3). Humility is the only appropriate posture when considering God.

Yet, this too is true: billions of humans have yearned for the presence, the guidance, and the love of God, and many have achieved powerful if

Rabbi Daniel Nevins is the Pearl Resnick Dean of The Rabbinical School of The Jewish Theological Seminary and is the chairman and a senior lecturer in its Department of Professional Skills. He serves on the executive council, joint placement commission, and law committee of the Rabbinical Assembly. Previously he served as senior rabbi of Adat Shalom Synagogue in Farmington Hills, Michigan.

fleeting experiences of that presence. Such experiences have the capacity to transform a life, a community, and an entire society. The yearning for God is a yearning for purpose, a sense that we are willed into existence for reasons mysterious, and that our lives, limited though they may be, may yet attain significance. As the psalmist says, "Taste and see how good the Lord is; happy the person who takes refuge in God" (Psalm 34:9). Our prayers guide us from helpless inadequacy to active searching. *Adon Olam* (Eternal Lord) takes us from God's transcendence over space-time (*b'li reishit, b'li tachlit*) to presence in our most vulnerable moments, at sleep and in death (*biyado afkid ruchi*). The nature of God is a mystery, but for many, the presence of God is a reality.

And more: we are not alone in our quest, but rather are enriched by traditions and communities of seekers who share our path and strengthen our purpose. The Jewish insistence on partnership in study (*chevruta*) and community in prayer (*minyan*) means that even the wisest and most spiritual seeker benefits from religious fellowship. In moments of weakness, community offers encouragement; in moments of presumption, community offers perspective and critique. The fellowship or covenant of seekers guides our pursuit of an elusive God. Perhaps this is why our mystical tradition refers to the most accessible facet of divinity as *k'nesset Yisrael*, the gathering of Israel. The same morning prayer that speaks of the insignificance of humanity proclaims, *Aval anachnu amkha b'nei b'ritekha*, "Yet we are Your people, children of Your covenant!"

What does it mean to be God's people, a people of covenant? *Eternal God, exceeding all measure or description, how shall we serve You?* This is no simple question, and there is no single answer. Every Shabbat, when we cease our own creative efforts and enter a contemplative frame of mind, we pray, "purify our hearts to serve You in truth." Perhaps we hope that this purification can be a magical gift from God, but Judaism offers a mechanism for pursuing this purpose: Torah and *mitzvot*. Study and worship, worship and study—there is no point in separating these aspects of our service. Through contemplation and action we integrate divine values into our lives, intending thus to purify our hearts so that we might serve God in truth. Sanctify us with your commandments, and grant our portion in your Torah, and purify our hearts to serve You in truth. Action leads to comprehension, which in turn leads to purity of the soul. This progression is at the very heart of Jewish practice.

"And now, O Israel, what does the Lord your God demand of you? Only this: to revere the Lord your God, to walk only in his paths, to love Him, and to serve the Lord your God with all your heart and soul" (Deuteronomy 10:12). There is an internal, emotional purpose that is paired with an external life of service. Walking in all of God's paths is a consequence of reverence and a condition for experiencing divine love. That is, a person must be reverent in order to subjugate the individual will and follow a path set by God. But in that walk, a person is able to love God, by perfecting his or her service until it becomes complete. As God instructs Abraham, "Walk in my ways and be blameless" (Genesis 17:1). Walking the path of divine command changes a person and makes him or her a reflection of God.

In Judaism this practice of walking with God is known by the term Halakhah (sacred pathway). Halakhah is often understood as a noun, as an established body of law. But this definition is inaccurate. Halakhah is a dynamic system, not a code. Even the halakhic codes composed by the great medieval sages Maimonides and Joseph Karo are surrounded by commentary like a garden path bordered by plants. Halakhah is a living, changing system, not a fixed and limited object. My deepest objection to Orthodoxy (within which I lived many productive years) is that it tends to personify (and thus objectify) God and that its concept of Halakhah is reactionary to modernity and thus rigid like scar tissue. These two errors are understandable—worshiping eternity is less satisfying than clinging to an anthropomorphic image of the Divine. Confidence that the law is established for all time is a comforting fiction even if it is undermined by every cacophonous page of the Talmud. Worshiping without truly understanding, and serving without certainty are frustrating religious postures, but they are honest and humble, and that should suffice.

Halakhah should be understood as the practice of walking with God. God's commands give structure to the walk, but so too do God's values as they are portrayed in our sacred literature. If God is said to be "good to all, His mercy is upon all his works" (Psalm 145:9), then our imitation of God had better be good and merciful. It has become customary to speak of meta-Halakhah, or the values that stand above or behind the law. Likewise, it is common to bifurcate Jewish literature into Halakhah and *aggadah*, law and lore, with the assumption that the latter corpus speaks to the moral essence of religion while the former is just a legalistic shell. This is a very ancient dichotomy; it was the core of Paul's critique of Judaism, and it has been resurrected many times by Jewish antinomians from the early Chasidim to the later reformers. So sustained has this critique been that some traditionalists have succumbed to its force and embraced a religious practice of meticulous conformity without religious comprehension.

Yet this alleged bifurcation has never been true to the best of Jewish literature and practice. Halakhah is deeply exegetical, and *aggadah* is grounded in legal norms. In the Talmud and many collections of Midrash, the two genres are intertwined and often indistinguishable. As Robert Cover wrote in his landmark article "Nomos and Narrative," societies are constantly generating law to reinforce their narratives of communal purpose, and narratives to give texture to their communal norms. Narrative (*aggadah*) is jurisgenerative, and law in turn creates identity.[1] Reading halakhic literature, especially in the genre of responsa, one is struck by the frequent citations of verses and *aggadot* that give context and significance to normative practice.

For many contemporary Jews, halakhic literature is literally incomprehensible. Its language, subject matter, and conventions are so thoroughly alien to any textual experience that a modern Jew is likely to have encountered that it takes years to become attuned to halakhic thinking. Moreover, the intensive study of particularistic norms is quite at odds with the religious conventions of our day, which value individual insight over communal worship. Nevertheless, halakhic thinking retains much appeal for several reasons.

Given our inability to know the mind of God, Halakhah offers the next best thing. It attests to what millennia of Jews have discerned to be the divine will. For all of its ambiguities, halakhic literature yields many distinct instructions. Eat this, and don't eat that. Say this, and don't say that. Pray like this, and not like that. Implicit in this discipline is the idea that following *mitzvot* (commandments) draws one closer to the realm of God, while committing *aveirot* (transgressions) distances one from the divine. Indeed, this belief is explicit in the blessing formula that attends many *mitzvot*: *asher kid'shanu b'mitzvotav*, "who has sanctified us through the commandments." Alas, there is no blessing formula for committing *aveirot*, though the pseudo-messiah Shabbetai Tzvi was said to have punned a blessing, *mattir issurim*, that God permits (former) prohibitions.

Furthermore, Halakhah gives us a practice of subjugating the will in service of our creator. Ideally, this practice leads to humility, though there is constant danger that such service can lead a person instead toward arrogance vis-à-vis other people whose observable service seems less rigorous. As long as a person remembers that our service is always imperfect compared to the transcendence of God, then the performance of *mitzvot* can be done with humility and integrity.

Finally, halakhic practice has the benefit of giving structure to a person's family and communal life. The predictable rituals and other practices mean that a practicing Jew can pick up and join nearly any community and has a reasonable chance of transferring the tradition to his or her children.

Given all of these benefits, halakhic practice is quite appealing. Yet because Halakhah is built upon a foundation of millennia, it contains a mixture of elements, some of which are sublime, others of which seem odd, and a few of which are frankly repulsive in a contemporary context. The same system that teaches us that humiliating a person is like murder also contains many norms and narratives that are deeply humiliating toward various classes of people. Gentiles, Jewish women, and people who identify as gay or lesbian are all subject to casually dismissive or destructive sentiments in halakhic literature, which are at times attached to hateful and hurtful practices.

Like a crushed soda can left beside a pristine mountain trail, hateful traditions embedded in halakhic literature can repulse the most devoted practitioner. Yet just as trash found in the wilderness invites a conscientious hiker to pick it up and pack it out, so too do hateful aspects of our ancient tradition (such as the command to annihilate the gentile population of Canaan) require attention and active response from contemporary practitioners. Indeed, it is the imperfection of all formulations of Judaism—past, present, and future—and the mechanisms for adjustment that keep the halakhic system vibrant and allow it to reflect the transcendent nature of God.

On Shabbat each week we sing the words *K'vodo malei olam, m'shartav sho'alim zeh lazeh ayei m'kom k'vodo*, "God's glory suffuses the universe, but His servants ask one another, where is the place of His glory?" This is the paradox of our faithful practice; we feel God's presence everywhere, yet we are unable to pinpoint it anywhere. Like the unseen and elusive God, our pursuit of holiness is ever beyond our reach. Rather than give up in frustration, we should recall yet again the words of Deuteronomy 10:12: "And now, O Israel, what does the Lord your God demand of you? Only this: to revere the Lord your God, to walk only in His paths, to love Him, and to serve the Lord your God with all your heart and soul." Reverence, active practice, and love. This is what God requires, and this is what Jews have tried to accomplish for millennia. The task is great, but God is said to forgive our failures so long as we keep trying to return. This is the path, the Halakhah, that a humble Jew can follow.

On This Sacred Ground

RABBI ELIYAHU STERN

"STILL NOT ALL OF YOU secularists wanted to overthrow the yoke of the law," bellowed the quasi-fictional character Reb Hersh Rasseyner at his nemesis, the twentieth-century novelist Chaim Grade. "Some grumbled that Judaism kept getting heavier all the time.... Lighten the weight a little, they said, ... but the more they lightened the burden the heavier the remainder seemed to them.... Anyone who thinks he can hold on to the basic principles and give up what he considers secondary is like a man who chops down the trunk of a tree and expects the root not to rot."[1] Reb Hersh's words stung his boyhood friend, Chaim, who had long ago lightened his burden but still held dear to his roots.

Reb Hersh believed there was only "one way out of this" fool's bargain, to "see the law as the only reality of life. Everything else is a dream. Even when a man understands rationally what he should do, he must never forget that before all else he should do it because the Law tells him to do so."

Reb Hersh offers a piercing critique and sober assessment of nineteenth- and twentieth-century attempts to reinterpret Halakhah. He scoffs at those from all Jewish denominations who tried to make

Rabbi Eliyahu Stern is assistant professor of modern Jewish intellectual and cultural history at Yale University. He is an American fellow of the Shalom Hartman Institute and received rabbinic ordination from Yeshiva University. He is currently writing a book on Elijah of Vilna.

Halakhah "fit into the modern world." For Hersch and his adherents, Halakhah offers a real philosophical and social alternative to the brutalities and vulgarities of Western materialism and nationalism. It paves a path, a narrow one indeed, for those who feel uneasy about the prospects of walking brazenly, head held high, with Philistines who long ago lost their moral compass.

Reb Hersh snickers at parents who thought they could tell their children to attend universities but leave their ideas about love and the good life in the library; go to Wall Street but keep its ethical shortcomings filed away in a cabinet; enjoy the social pleasures of bourgeois life but only bring home a Jew of the opposite sex. For Reb Hersh, Halakhah is countercultural, requiring total dedication to its statutes. Halakhah is the grammar that makes the universe intelligible for those whose canon begins with tractate *B'rakhot* and ends with *Uktzin*, for those whose livelihood is the study of Torah, for those whose courts are presided over by rabbinic authorities, and for those who go to the wedding canopy at eighteen. Such a *nomos* guarantees more than mere meaning; it takes guts and offers spiritual glory.

While secular Judaism continues to be consumed by the natural selection processes of assimilation, Halakhah has faired much better, weathering the storm of Charles Darwin and blossoming in communities throughout the world. Still, the overwhelming majority of Jews today are neither practicing nor invested in Halakhah. For most, Reb Hersch's world is simply too sexist and secluded to be a real option.

However, unlike our parents, most Jews today are neither accepting nor rebelling against Halakhah. This generation was raised by those who long ago ripped apart the sacred canopy protecting and limiting horizons to a monolithic ghettoized Judaism. Most Jews today inhabit a world, at least in theory, that is full of choices. We feel no sentimentality or guilt toward not being accepted or respected by Reb Hersh.

For most Jews of this generation, the roots of their tradition have finished rotting, allowing them to sit on a hollowed stump pondering what might be replanted on these sacred grounds. For those who don't see the lifestyle, social structures, and relationship models of the fervent Orthodox as options but who likewise don't see Halakhah through the jaundiced or sentimental eyes of our grandparents, what meaning, if any, might Halakhah have to offer?

Approaching this question anew entails distinguishing Halakhah from its common nineteenth- and twentieth-century definition as law. Halakhah and law are two distinct worldviews with radically different goals. Halakhah promotes a specific type of free-choosing, God-centered, and morally responsible individual. State law's chief objective, for better or worse, is to create order and, at best, serve as a ground to mediate conflicting claims of the right and the good. The two systems, if Halakhah can even be called such, are radically different, baring only the kind of superficial overlap that the untrained eye could mistake for similarity. The legal theorist Ronald Dworkin would never compare himself to Moses or Maimonides, and neither should we. When seen as law, Halakhah is reduced to a system of rules and regulations. However, Halakhah has never been a modern system of law, whose purpose was merely the ordering of a community or following the wanton dictates of a ruler or king. Certainly those who embrace its minutia do not relate to it in such terms. For them, Halakhah is not some annoying governing system comprised of bureaucratic stop signs and red lights; it is what gives meaning to their lives.

Instead of encountering Halakhah as a form of coercive state law, we ought to see it as a commandment or perhaps, more accurately, as a something that "compels" us to take seriously our surroundings, our relationships, and the moral implications of our actions. Such a worldview works against social experiences that numb our emotional and moral sensibilities, that make us forget ourselves. Indeed, we have been exceptional at accomplishing such self-defeating goals. For how much room is there really for us to assert ourselves in a world in which we are expected to be enrolled in school until we are in our late twenties, hold a job that takes up the majority of our time until our seventies, and raise families from age thirty until the day we are buried? At very early stages in our lives, expectations are hoisted upon us, determining where we live, with whom, and under what circumstances. Schools lead to jobs, which lead to mating partners, which lead to more kids, which lead to more schools. It is easy to see how such a life slowly divests us of choice, agency, and the ability to effect personal and social redemption.

From Maimonides to Hermann Cohen, Jews assert that the concept of *b'chirah chofshit* (choice) is the foundation upon which religious action gains moral value. In his code of law, *Mishneh Torah*, Maimonides states that to be considered a true penitent a person must be placed in the same position and under the same conditions as when he or she sinned with nothing preventing him or her from committing the same transgression. According to Maimonides, actions gain religious meaning only when done out of *b'chirah chofshit*. The seemingly pious veneer of Maimonides' argument quickly disappears when we look at its implications. Imagine if a thief could only be truly rehabilitated if he were placed in front of a bank at 3 a.m. with no guards or locks on the door and no surveillance camera looking down upon him. It is only under such circumstances that Maimonides could envision the thief being truly forgiven.

Maimonides' ideas can be found already in rabbinic literature regarding the rationale for why Joseph is regarded as righteous. Joseph is lying in bed with Potiphar's wife, yet his lust and desire do not overwhelm his moral senses. Even under political and physical duress, Joseph asserts that another option is available. While Judaism regards Joseph as a *tzaddik* (righteous person), a state-sanctioned legal system would never be able to give any medal or bestow any honor for his actions.

Perhaps a less racy and more practical example of what I am suggesting can be found in the mishnah traditionally read every Friday night:

> If one extinguishes a lamp because he is afraid of the offi-
> cers of the government, or of robbers, or of an evil spirit,
> or in order that a sick person may be able to sleep, he is
> free. If he does this, however, to prevent damage to the

lamp, or to save the oil or the wick, he is culpable. R. Jose
declares the man free even in the latter cases, excepting [if
he extinguished the lamp to save the wick], for in that case
he caused a cinder to be formed. (*Mishnah Shabbat* 2:5)

Shabbat has a specific purpose. It is not just a random time in which
Simon says freeze. It beseeches us to stop tinkering with the environment for our needs. It screams, "Stop trying to get everything down to a
science!" Leave the world of economic gain and mass manipulation. Let
ourselves and our surroundings be, just as we are, just for a few minutes.

The idea of rest is not a legal category; it is a telos. Thus, if a person
is faced with a situation in which the rules of Shabbat are preventing
him or her from experiencing the overarching goals of Shabbat, he or
she is permitted, in a sense, to break from the normally prescribed
forms of behavior for achieving "rest" and adopt other practices to pro-
mote those goals. In some cases this may lead to more restrictions. In
other instances, it might lead to less. The point here is not to allow people to break or lighten the load of Shabbat, but rather to ensure that
Shabbat achieves itself.

Blowing out candles on Shabbat is not normally part of a Shabbat
lifestyle, but if such a law leads, say, to a person sitting alone in his or
her room depressed for endless hours on a Friday night (as most inter-
preters understand the term "evil spirit"), to the point that his or her
experience of Shabbat is fundamentally comprised, then the person is
commanded to entertain the possibility of taking a spiritual risk. There
are few rules and guidelines for something as vague as depression.
When faced with such a situation, the person needs to ask, is this
merely another attempt to manipulate and control or is my loneliness
or physical sickness preventing me from celebrating? Halakhah forces
the person to confront the situation and be honest with how he or she
feels, to explore what needs and aspects of his or her life are not being
met. It demands that in each moment a person make conscious choices
as to how he or she would like to act and be prepared to accept the
repercussions of those actions.

Some would be quick to point out that regarding Shabbat, folios upon folios have been written to limit, define, and explain the contours of this mishnah. The truth of the matter is that theoretically, law's empire can reach ad infinitum, detailing every single exception to every rule. However, Halakhah is not a legal system as in the one described by the modern Jewish philosopher Rabbi Joseph B. Soloveitchik in *Halakhic Man*, or in the set of folk practices as claimed by the Reconstructionist ideologue Rabbi Mordecai Kaplan and the modern rabbi-scholar Robert Gordis in *Judaism as Civilization* and *Minhag America* (respectively), or in the coercive-heteronymous law rejected by Reform theologians. Rather, it is an outlook and a lifestyle geared toward life fulfillment, cultivation of a more refined self, and the redemption of the world.

While the case of blowing out the candles on Shabbat highlights the way Halakhah engenders a consciousness of choice for humans, the case of *b'rakhot r'iyah* (sight-based blessings) expresses the way Halakhah heightens a person's awareness toward his or her surroundings, relationships, and experiences. These blessings cover a broad swath of human experience, including memorializing space, greeting friends, and marking wondrous moments. These blessings were not instituted for the purposes of transcending or sublimating the present, or to be mumbled over and over again throughout the day with the hope of appeasing a sycophantic God. They remind us of the infrastructure of human existence, moments of happiness and loss, engaging human beings, experiencing fully both banal and remarkable happenings.

Scholars note that prior to these blessings being listed in the ninth chapter of tractate *B'rakhot*, their recitation was frowned upon by those who circumscribed God's name to Temple activities. Following the destruction of the Temple, however, the Rabbis instituted these blessings with the hope of reminding people that godliness and leading a meaningful life were not about going to three-times-a-year prayer events. Rather, they were about the godliness in what rests before their eyes.

Whether standing in front of God, a child, a spouse, a business associate, or simply the mirror, the need arises to justify our actions and undertakings. Merely following what the law prescribes fails to guarantee a quiet conscience or provide a valid excuse for our behavior. Though our actions might be justified in some robotic bureaucratic legal structure, such forms of idolatry and fetish have little to do with Halakhah's emphasis on morality, human flourishing, or the attribute of mercy. When Halakhah becomes simply a matter of do's and don'ts, it can all too often seem ethically senseless, sexist, and disturbingly ascetic. Each individual must come to terms with what he or she is ultimately willing to take responsibility for. Imagine if Esther had not slept with Ahasuerus because the law said she should not. What would have happened to the Jewish People? Imagine if Phineas had let formal legal requirements determine his moral horizon. While Esther's decision was depicted as being objectively correct and Phineas's response was greeted with much more caution, their antinomian actions were received positively because both individuals recognized that Halakhah was not a coercive legal system but rather a commandment rooted in choice, forcing individuals at every moment to be responsible for their actions.

My point is not that Halakhah should be *an* option in a person's life. When we speak of Halakhah as having a specific response to a specific situation, it ceases to become a lifestyle and turns into a legal system. For Halakhah to have meaning, it must become The Option that creates the conditions of possibility to all options. It must become the process (as opposed to a system of law that forces and coerces) that restores dignity and choice to the individual and gives honor and recognition to the spiritual and moral values we hold dear and essential. Halakhah must be something that reminds us at all times that we must pick and choose and take responsibility for every action.

A halakhic outlook must seep into nook and cranny not as it does for Reb Hersh—to act as a buffer against this world—but rather the opposite; namely, to make us more attached to this world, to force us to be cognizant of what we are doing and the hard choices that sometimes follow and, when need be, allow us to break with traditional modes of behavior. When our tradition tells us that a person is required to bless the good as well as the bad, it is not just making a statement about

God's omnipotence, but reminding us that there is no realm that is empty or devoid of meaning-making moments. Godliness is not located in foxholes, synagogues, temples, and study halls. It is located in the lives we choose to lead.

Chaim Grade's and Reb Hersch's debate circled around who was the rightful custodian of Judaism. Today we find ourselves in a very different position. I do not mean that most Jews don't feel any responsibility for the upkeep of Judaism, but rather that most human beings don't feel any responsibility for anything. "Whatever" has replaced "*I care*" in our social vocabulary. While Halakhah may not be a panacea for the rehabilitation of the individual, it calls upon us to appreciate our lives and take responsibility for the world we create.

THE GOD IN
BETWEEN

The Radical Divinity

RABBI TAMAR ELAD-APPELBAUM

ON TUESDAY NIGHT, the eighteenth of Av 5761, August 9th, 2001, three uniformed Israeli Defense Forces (IDF) officers knocked on the door of our home in Jerusalem. At six o'clock earlier that evening, my brother Nadav, a combat soldier in an élite paratrooper unit, had fallen in action in the Hevron area, just one month before his twentieth birthday. The three officers said strange words to me and escorted me to my parents' home. All along, I spoke with Nadav and my God with eyes closed, asking to reverse this terrible decree. I addressed the Heart of the World with a desperate plea; crawled with my words to the foot of the Throne of Mercy, begging that my brother's soul be returned to its mortal coil. I promised that I would not reveal the secret of this little resurrection of the dead being made between us. I did not open my eyes for even one moment, so as not to lose the thread. When we arrived at my parents' home, I stumbled up the steps to the door. I thrust my hand on the doorknob, my insides trembling, and paused and asked for one last private

Rabbi Tamar Elad-Appelbaum is interim rabbi serving alongside Rabbi Gordon Tucker at Temple Israel Center in White Plains, New York. She is the designated associate dean of the Schechter Rabbinical Seminary in Jerusalem; former rabbi of congregation Magen Avraham Omer in the Israeli Negev; former vice president of the Rabbinical Assembly in Israel; serves on the boards of several organizations working to achieve religious pluralism in Israel; and is a writer of contemporary Hebrew poetry and thought. She lives in Jerusalem with her husband and two daughters.

moment. The three officers stood aside. My husband, Yossi, held my hand, and I wept some final words of prayer in my brother's name: "God, the soul which you have given me is pure. You created it, You formed it, You breathed life into it, You preserve it within me, and You shall take it from me and return it to me in the world-to-come. So long as the soul is within me I give thanks to You, Lord God and God of my fathers, Master of all deeds, Lord of all souls. Blessed are You, who returns the soul to lifeless bodies." I did not move; nothing moved. In the darkness of that Tuesday, whose goodness escaped me, I awaited an answer, but my beloved had passed away. My brother was dead and would not return. I saw him in my mind's eye, handsome and smiling. I said in my heart, "The Holy One blessed be He creates worlds and destroys them," and opened the door.

From a Theology of Stability to a Theology of "Rings of the Ark"

If God is Absolute Being, embodying the totality of time and place, the absolute basis of unconditional existence, as opposed to the limited life and capacity of the human being, it is reasonable to arrive at an image whose power is based upon perfect stability. And indeed, echoes of such thought can be found in various sources, as in the words of Kohelet: "I realize, too, that whatever God has brought to pass will recur evermore: nothing can be added to it and nothing taken from it—and God has brought to pass that men revere Him" (Ecclesiastes 3:14). This voice, identifying God with the fixed and stable order of the world, requires a pattern of human behavior based upon constant obedience, so that man might not injure the divine order.

But there is another voice found throughout the tradition, one that identifies divine guidance with change and upheaval. Thus, for example, in the words of Rabbi Yehudah and Rabbi Abbahu:

> Rabbi Yehudah bar Simon said: It does not say "it was evening" but "*and* it was evening" [Genesis 1:5]. From this we infer that time and order existed prior to creation. Rabbi

> Abbahu taught that He created worlds and destroyed them,
> until He created these ... "and behold, it was very good
> [Genesis 1:31]." (*Genesis Rabbah* 3:7)

From the seemingly superfluous *vav consecutive* ("and") in the account
of the first evening of creation, these two sages infer that time, the
world, and history existed even before our world came into existence,
attributing to God a history of creation and destruction that ended with
God's dwelling in a world that God saw as good.

They are not the only voices of this kind. To a large extent, these are
the voices of the Bible and of the Sages generally, which caution
humankind not to find comfort in a supposedly stable God. Divine
existence, say those voices, is not equivalent to stability, and stability is
not promised to humankind. On the contrary, God's presence in the
world is the fixed presence of change. This is reflected symbolically in
the words of Rav Yosef, who describes the duality of the Divine Taber-
nacle: "'[The tablets] that you smashed, and you shall deposit them [in
the ark]' [Deuteronomy 10:2]—this teaches us that the tablets and the
broken pieces of the tablets rested together in the ark" (BT *Bava Batra*
14b). The ark of the covenant, the very heart of the sanctuary, carries
within itself both the law and its "breaking." The same is reflected in
the homes of God's beings: When a Jew attaches a *mezuzah* to the
entrance of his or her home, he or she recites in paradoxical language
"to affix a *mezuzah*" (*Shulchan Arukh, Yoreh De'ah* 289)—to affix something with movement, the word *mezuzah* being cognate to *t'zuzah*,
"movement" . Like the sanctuary, the *mezuzah* on the home of the Jew
is a sign of both fixity and change. This idea is also mirrored in the
house of God. In describing the construction of the ark, the Bible
specifically dwells upon the rings of the ark and the staves, which are
not to be removed (Exodus 25:15). The ark must always be ready to be
moved, for the God of Israel is a God of journeys, who calls upon Abraham to move about, and Abraham's offspring to follow in his wake. The
God of Israel is the God of movement to the Promised Land. The God
of Israel is the God of change and revolution, the radical divinity.

The Radical Divinity

Divinity is the radical force that moves the entire cosmos, from one end of the world to the other, and the goal of the Jewish story is to serve witness to this. Thus, in the creation story, God took the world of chaos, broke down both its concepts and its reality, and rebuilt them in the form of heaven and earth, luminaries, plants, and living beings, finally establishing humankind in God's image and likeness. The story of the beginning of the world is a story of deconstruction, of chaos, and of new creation by means of the Divine. The same follows from the story of Noah and the Flood—breaking down, rebuilding, and reassembly of humankind; the tower of Babel—breaking down and reconstructing language and the attitude toward life; Abraham—breaking down and reconstructing ethics; Egypt—destroying slavery and subjugation and building within the people a new reality of freedom. Numerous biblical stories are characterized by the tension between creation and destruction in God's world, by the quest for that same intensely sought "and it was good" (even bodily changes, such as circumcision, are related to this). This includes not only stories of the past, but also the vision for the future. Prophetic visions denounce the rot of unethical behavior and sketch upon the religious horizon the possibility of a new reality better suited to the dwelling place of the God of justice and mercy, as is implied in the words of the prophet Isaiah: "For behold! I am creating a new heaven and a new earth; the former things shall not be remembered, they shall never come to mind" (Isaiah 65:17). The *Tanakh* is filled with stories of the radical God, who breaks down reality and creates a new one from its ashes, smashes humankind's dreams of an idyll and creates another in its place. But the miraculous nature of divine radicalism lies in the fact that every act of breaking down is simultaneously a new putting together. The Divine never breaks things down merely to leave reality in ruins; rather, God takes things apart in order to create a new and better order: "He did not create it a waste, but formed it for habitation" (Isaiah 45:18).

God, therefore, is the most anti-nomistic element in reality. That same Divinity who sustains the world constantly undermines its stability. In a single "Let there be light," an entire order was created as well as its fixed hidden shadow of potential change. God's very existence dictates a history of constant flux: the evolution of ideas, ideals, and revolutions. When God brings forth knowledge within humankind—that is to say, the power of cognition and of creativity—humankind is destined to inherit and nullify anew its god, its world, and its own consciousness. Thus, humankind and God are transformed into partners in the secret order of the world and in its constant change.

Jewish Religiosity

What should Jews do in the well-ordered but unstable world of the Divine? How should we behave, when our longing for the living God comes from our amazed contemplation of the wonders of the ordered world, and simultaneously from the turbulence that bursts forth and undercuts everything known to us? The image of God is reflected in the image of us; order and change are interwoven with one another; the tablets and their broken fragments are placed together in the ark, and in the world. It seems as though the Jewish service of God springs forth two deeply opposite yet complementary tracks. The purpose of one track is to restrain us; that of the other, to familiarize us with the radical experience. The first track is that of acceptance of the yoke of the commandments; the second, that of Torah study and prayer.

The entire object of *mitzvot* (commandments), the first avenue in the service of God, is to place a millstone upon the necks of God's created beings and to restrain us. The system of *mitzvot* is a warning to us not to topple the existing order. Every *mitzvah* is intended as an exercise in modesty imposed upon us: to humble our creative souls so as not to interfere in reality and to observe the beauty of the order around us. *Mitzvot* enable a glimpse at this order and the institutions that protect it, serving as faithful gatekeepers. The yoke of the commandments also offers a glimpse into the depths of the opposition to this order that ferments within our souls. Only when we confront both of these can we grow into the image of God, dormant within ourselves, and limit ourselves sufficiently so as to awaken new world concepts within our thought. The power of restraint found within the *mitzvot* is most clearly reflected in the act of donning *tefillin* (phylacteries). A person who observes people putting on *tefillin* sees a congregation of Jews who rein in their spirit while whispering words of love to their creator.

Against that, the study of Torah and the act of prayer serve as gradual exercises in the radical experience, beginning with study and culminating in prayer. The person who studies Torah is required to learn the panoply of voices that preceded his or her own life and at the same time has the religious obligation to add his or her own unique voice to theirs. To quote the words of Rabbi Eliezer Ashkenazi the Physician:

> Do not be alarmed when you find the words of the great
> ones in the land who disagree, but search out and examine,
> for it is for this that you were created and given intelligence
> from above, and this will assist you. And if you wish to be
> of benefit to those who come after you as well, take from
> your own ideas and record them in a book in ink.[1]

The system of Torah study is the bridge between the two channels of service to God: it requires that humankind restrain its creative power in order to accept the yolk of the communal language of Torah, while at the same time stimulating its creative, exegetical power. The concept of *machloket* (debate) embedded in Jewish study is the realm of the in-between (*karm'lit*) resolved through an opening (*tzurat hapetach*), serving as a bridge between the realm of the public (*r'shut harabbim*) and that of the private (*r'shut hayachid*). The world of Torah study, then, is like a pendulum swaying between the reality of the text and the open possibilities of shared interpretations. As formulated by Rabbi Avraham Isaac Kook in his commentary on the prayer book:

> The multiplicity of opinions that accompanies the variety
> of people and of students is precisely that which enriches

> wisdom and causes it to expand.... For it is impossible to
> build the future building of peace, save by those selfsame
> influences that seem to be jousting with one another.[2]

Peace is therefore increased in the world by the broadest possible involvement in the concept of controversy, whose intra-Jewish use is no more than a preparation for the revolutionary worldwide use intended for it. Building peace is not merely an embodiment of political agreement; it also deepens the flexibility of the mind and the place of all creatures of the world, that they not be destroyed. The building of peace must come from the division among peoples, each one redeeming the exile of the other from the theological bastions in which they have been placed. "In all of My sacred mount, nothing evil or vile shall be done; for the land shall be filled with knowledge of God, as water covers the sea" (Isaiah 11:9).

But beyond the study house there is prayer, the pinnacle of the second channel of divine service. The worshiping person knows that he never leaves prayer as he went into it. In his longing to speak with the Living God, he casts off all restraints and becomes immersed in the creative power within himself. He calls out and beseeches, he breaks down reality within his mind in order to bring about a better one. When he is done, he emerges a different person. This follows from the prayer of Hannah, who demanded to be relieved of her protracted barrenness into the reality of new life. It is therefore not surprising that the Sages saw her as the source of inspiration for all matters of prayer (BT *B'rakhot* 31a). The dictates of prayer create a community of people who beg for their own lives and for the world, like paupers gathering sheaves in the field. Alongside one another, they uncover the inner desire of their existence and sketch its contours before their creator so that it may be realized. It is not easy to bow down and to ask, but prayer—*avodah* in the language of the Sages—is that place in which a congregation of believers is called upon to cast off their attachment to certainty and to seek "and it was good" in the world of "perhaps." It is not surprising that Chasidim invested so much effort in preparation for prayer and feared that they might die in the moment of prayer, like Rabbi Uri of Strelisk ("The Angel") who, before going to pray, "would gather his household together and take leave of his wife and children."[3] Or, as formulated in the *Testament of the Baal Shem Tov*:

> It is a great kindness from God, may He be blessed, that a person lives after he has prayed. For in the natural course of things he ought to have died, for he used up all of his vital energy in prayer, for he expended so much power in prayer because of the intentions that he makes.[4]

Between the praises of divine order and lawfulness found in *P'sukei D'zimra*, and the new light planted on the path to the *Sh'ma* and the *Amidah*, between their mouths and their innards, bound in *tefillin*, Jewish worshipers dig within their world and commit themselves to create something that reflects their goodness. One must add that the power of love is like the power of prayer—in both of them there is revealed the secret of redemption.

The Radical Act

These channels of service to God—*mitzvot*, Torah study, and prayer— are like projections onto which one holds fast while climbing a mountain. The religious experience is not complete without all three and the tension among them. But that is not all. From *mitzvot*, from Torah study, and from prayer, one must go out into the streets, the place of partnership in the divine act.

Rabbi Hiyya bar Abba drew a connection between the worshiper and the street, saying that "a man should always pray in a building with windows" (BT *B'rakhot* 31a). In portraying the religious architecture of the Jewish tradition, Rabbi Hiyya states that there can be no prayer without a window upon the world. Therefore, under no circumstances can the experience of the religious person be encompassed by obedience and its derivations alone. Through *mitzvot*, Torah study, and prayer, a person trains him- or herself to engage with the larger, ever-changing world. The pinnacle of religious experience is a radical, creative act: daring to see faults in God's world, and to outline, with modesty and delicacy, a new horizon.

Faith is a double pact: on one hand, not to undermine the order of life, and on the other, not to unravel the connection of participation in the divine creation. These two are the twin forces of the tree of life and the tree of knowledge that were in the Garden. Faith (*emunah*) is the art of absolute loyalty (*ne'emanut*) to God through the yoke of observance and the practice found in study and prayer. Faith is the art of refusal (*mi'un*) to become acclimated to a reality that is not good enough as well as the radical religious act of standing up against injustice and corruption.

The believing person is a constant climber. His or her life is a constant movement toward "and it was good," toward a partnership of destiny with the God of the world and with primordial climbers like Abraham, Moses, and other revolutionary radical leaders. But like Moses, every religious person must throughout his or her entire life climb Mount Nebo, never to enter into the Promised Land.

Radical Divinity and Zionism

We who have the privilege of living in a generation of Jews who saw the building of the State of Israel know well this tension between entering the Promised Land and yet standing on Nebo. With our own eyes we see a miraculous state that is on the verge of catastrophe. So much pain wafts out of the frozen Israelite spirit upon the renewal of Jewish life in Zion. Might it be possible for us, on our part, to think of the two channels of religious service—restraint and creativity—as two historical stages in the development of Israel?

The first sixty years of the State of Israel were invested entirely in the first channel of divine service, in restraining the spiritual and creative powers of the Jewish soul. But in today's State of Israel there are hundreds and thousands of secular and religious Jews engaged in studying Torah, thereby bringing our state closer to the beginning of a recognition of the second channel of divine service—that of Torah study and prayer, of radical creativity.

And so, that is our mission. The task of the rabbis in Israel during the coming generations will therefore be preparing the Jewish heart to attain the summit of the second channel in the service of God, that of prayer, establishing the synagogue as a religious space of the greatest importance, making poetry and music central to the creation of a heterophonic religiosity (in a world whose melodies too often range between the homophonic and cacophony), deepening the power of the Israeli community by connecting the wills of individuals with one another, thereby cementing anew the relationship to the Zionist concept. For the Jewish path as a whole prepares for the redemption of figure from image, for the redemption of the living God from those dead vessels in which God has placed the divine self, "a king held captive in the tresses" (Song of Songs 7:6). For in truth, there is no redemption without movement. We must hold fast, with all our strength, to the cliff's projections and climb up into the mists of the Israeli Nebo, where we will take part in the ongoing embodiment of the partnership of humankind and God in history.

∽

Like flowing water, it is impossible to take hold of the mystery of God. Like love, it is beyond apprehension. The tremendous power of life within the realms of the universe gushes out of the Divine One. God— a non-place, non-time—could have elicited fear, violence, and silence, yet God comforts and calls upon us to blossom. God loves us with a great love, giving us the power to come and go with God in strength, for the service of God is the supreme educational space in reality. God does not reveal anything, but demands us to discover the things from within. Without depriving the scholar of his or her knowledge, while completely casting aside the narcissistic needs of the divine teacher, the service of God enables humankind to test its abilities to the extreme, so that two independent partners may always exist within the space of world creation: humankind and God of the universe. And we do hear and respond to one another. From the fear of death and the longing for a living God, we bring forth our life, our time and place, our society and context. From moment to moment the reflection of God touches our reflection and awakens faith in us. Take notice, says God. Take notice, I repeat to myself. Not to despair, not to stumble, not to wither. To open door after door to the living God, to open it within myself and in reality, door after door, hope after hope.

I wish to thank Rabbi Yehonatan Chipman for his translation of this article into English and Renana Rosenbloom for her insightful editorial comments.

How I Came to
Theology, or Didn't

RABBI DANIEL M. BRONSTEIN, PHD

TOWARD THE CLOSE of the Marx Brothers classic *A Night at the Opera*, Chico, disguised as a Russian aviator, dissembles to a welcoming party how he and his brothers journeyed to American shores:

> The first time we started, we get-a halfway across when we run out-a gasoline and we gotta go back. Then I take-a twice as much gasoline. This time we-a just about to land—maybe three feet—when whaddya think? We run out-a gasoline again and a-back we go again to get-a more gas. This time I take plenty gas. Well, we get-a halfway over when what-a you think happened? We forgot-a the aeroplane. So we gotta sit down and we talk it over. Then

Rabbi Daniel M. Bronstein, PhD, serves as congregational scholar at Congregation Beth Elohim in Brooklyn, New York. He received his PhD in Jewish history from The Jewish Theological Seminary of America and was ordained at Hebrew Union College–Jewish Institute of Religion. Rabbi Bronstein has taught in a variety of forums, from synagogues to the Association for Jewish Studies, the Center for Jewish History, and The Jewish Theological Seminary. His writing has been featured in popular and academic publications, including *The Forward*, *JEWCY*, *Central Conference of American Rabbis Journal*, and *Jews and American Popular Culture* and *The Cambridge Dictionary of Jewish Religion, History, and Culture*.

> I get a great idea. We no take-a gasoline. We no take-a the
> aeroplane. We take a steamship. And that, friends, is how
> we fly across the ocean.

Written and delivered for profane rather than sacred purpose, Chico's
voyage homily nevertheless serves as a metaphor for a variety of life
experiences. How often in trying to get from one place to another we
try one route over and over again, only to fall short and, in the end,
finally arrive at the intended location by completely unexpected means.
My own encounter, if not collision, with the varieties of Jewish theology has been like Chico's hit-and-miss excursion. Expecting to arrive at
concrete answers in one manner, I instead found structure and substance from a more obvious source. From time immemorial people of
all creedal colors have labored over what have been given the blanket
designation of theological questions: the nature, or lack thereof, of
divinity; the question of human suffering; the demarcation, if even discovery, of goodness and evil.

In my private life and as part of my training, I have examined the
usual suspects, from ancient and medieval philosophers and modern
Jewish theologians. To be clear, I have never racked up any great academic achievement or original ideas in the course of such musings,
and I still deeply regret being a particularly annoying student in some
of my philosophy and theology classes during the course of rabbinic
school. One such incident during a commentaries course stands out
in particular. After asking several, ultimately unimportant theological
questions about a specific passage, my teacher in turn responded with
an old joke chronicling an exchange between another student who
was continually asking his teacher theological questions. The punch
line of the joke was the teacher's response: "Ah shaddup and daven
Minchah." It was good advice. More often than not, it is more important to be doing rather than talking. And certainly the Sages thought
so; a quick scan of *Pirkei Avot*—not to mention many other sources—
reveals more than one instance of the tradition's preference for action
over talk.

Maybe by the Renaissance but certainly by the Enlightenment, Jewish theologians have attempted to re-explain, if not re-justify, Judaism according to the intellectual demands of modernity. But I would argue that the outcome of these efforts has been reminiscent of the legend about the Dutch boy engaged in the impossible task of trying to cork the fissures appearing endlessly in a leaky embankment; after plugging one leak another drip would spring forth. Many theologians—far more intelligent and far more articulate than I—have also faced an analogous albeit intellectual process. While trying to address old theological problems, theologians have found themselves creating new ones. However brilliant, theologies are always broken down, chewed up, and discarded. Postmodern deconstruction has unmasked the many strategies of modern thought as mere systems of ideological self-justification. But unlike philosophies of the former, postmodern thought has often evaded addressing questions of moral absolutes, either denying the existence or dismissing the need for genuine moral boundaries, thus transforming issues of ethics to constructs. The hermeneutics of late twentieth-century postmodern thought did a fine and sometimes necessary job of exploding conventional Western modes of thinking for me, including those of modern Jewish theology, but ultimately left me dissatisfied and without grounding in any attempts to understand the big theological issues. In and out of the classroom, and even when I was the proverbial three feet from the answers, I still found it necessary to return to my starting point. Finally, I ended up "sailing" rather than "flying" in trying to address and reach conclusions about theological questions.

What does this mean? I know that I have some basic beliefs and am entirely cognizant that, unlike Paul who got his answers on the road to Damascus, my core beliefs are informed by my upbringing, personal experiences, and education. I will concede from the very beginning that my worldview is subjective. Still, I insist on asserting the existence of moral absolutes alongside ethical ambiguities in the human experience. I know that I believe in a radically transcendent God who is covenanted in a unique fashion to *Am Yisrael* and moreover believe that the House of Israel is obligated to serve as a "light unto the nations" (Isaiah 49:6). I likewise have no doubts that all of humanity is created in the image of the Divine. As did my ancestors, I believe that being Jewish is about carrying out commitments, retaining boundaries while also staying open to outside insights and remembering our heritage. I don't think this is much of a theology, and I realize that all of the above is unoriginal. Alternatively, there is no theology, Jewish or otherwise, that can withstand the scrutiny of some basic questions such as the nature of the Divine or the existence of suffering and/or evil. For me, the one constant is Torah. And I can only concur with the nineteenth-century Talmudist and ethicist Yisrael Salanter's teaching that even while we do "not have the capacity to apprehend true wisdom, absolutely purified and divorced from human emotion" the Torah enables us to "make judgments according to the human intellect."[1]

By Torah I mean the obligation to engage in Jewish learning in its myriad forms whether traditional or contemporary. For me, Torah, whether Written or Oral, is enriched and strengthened by modern disciplines such as the study of history and culture, language and literature, including non-Jewish sources, and, furthermore, the interaction of the two. The very act as well as the results of learning also serve to preserve and to keep us rooted in the best approaches of our ancestors. Torah fortifies and enhances my awe of the Divine. Traditional Torah learning especially maintains and enhances my bond with other branches of Jewry with whom I may disagree about the interpretation of the tradition and practice of Judaism. *Talmud Torah* is for me as much a form of worship as is the act of prayer. Last but not least, when properly performed, the act of learning, properly directed, furthers my particular commitments to the Jewish People while engendering further service to humanity as a whole, even while refining my personal conduct.

Talmud Torah k'neged kulam, the Sages explained long before Marx or the Marx Brothers, Kant or Foucault: the "learning of Torah is equal to all other *mitzvot*." Here I would return to Salanter, whom I believe to be of unique value for our time. As he formulated the task, the study and teaching of Torah is the "primary reason that study is [even] greater than the deed, for study engenders the deed."[2] All the more so, the act of learning Torah is vital to contemporary Jewry, whether traditional, modern, postmodern or post-postmodern, because as Salanter teaches, *talmud Torah* directs us to employ "incisive logic to innovate new laws and reconcile conflicting opinions,"[3] key tools in facing old questions and contemporary ethical challenges. Learning creates and maintains the awe of heaven and consciousness of the earth. Torah must always be carried out in the earthly realm of human life. Here especially, Salanter offers a useful term: *y'di'as hatorah*. More than simply being knowledge of the Torah, *y'di'as hatorah*, he explains, is the process of genuinely internalizing learning. Truly internalizing Torah sets in motion the ability for all of us to express and apply our knowledge in all of our interactions with others.

Discussing the significance of Torah, Rabbi Alexandri taught that learning for its own sake "makes peace in the household above and in the household below," while Rabbi Levi asserted that Torah "brings redemption nearer" (BT *Sanhedrin* 99b). Peacemaking in heaven and earth and progress toward redemption are no small matters. To get there we sometimes need to sail rather than fly.

The Theology of the *In-Between*

Benjamin Sax, PhD

The one no less than the other was God's doing.
—Ecclesiastes 7:14

We find in the Palestinian Talmud in *Hagigah* 2:1 the following statement:

> This teaching is like two paths, one of fire and one of
> snow. If one inclines to this side, one dies by fire; to that
> side, and one dies by snow. What should one do? Walk in
> the middle.

This theological balance, one between Halakhah and *aggadah*, or
one between *ma'aseh b'reishit* (the account of creation; physics, science)
and *ma'aseh merkavah* (the account of Ezekiel's chariot; metaphysics,
philosophy, mysticism), or simply one between competing worldviews,
is replete within Jewish history. Sigmund Freud once remarked Jews
possess multiple passports—that is to say, they inhabit and balance

---

Benjamin Sax, PhD, is assistant professor in the Department of Religion
and Culture and director of the Malcolm and Diane Rosenberg Program in
Judaic Studies at Virginia Tech. He received his MA from the Hebrew University of Jerusalem and PhD from the University of Chicago.

myriad cultural and intellectual realities, which have poignant ethical and theological implications. The sanguine kinship of Jews worldwide, at times celebrated as a *Schicksalsgemeinschaft* ("a community of destiny") in the modern world is intimately and inexorably bound, what the French existentialist Jean-Paul Sartre mused, to people "whose face[s] we don't recognize." Jews, whether committed to an obdurate orthodoxy or to experimenting with more flexible, modern, avant-garde Jewish movements, experience a world where identity, culture, and theological speculation is ever-changing. Defining oneself through others is a central characteristic of Jewish experience. Making sense of this experience is the task of Jewish theology.

When asked about his Judaism, Woody Allen responded, "I am Jewish, but with an explanation." Even though Allen was not drawing on the rabbinic axiom above explicitly, he reminds us of the aphorism in BT *Chullin* 18b that states, "Every river has its course." I feel the same way. When asked about what I believe, I feel the very question bespeaks a cultural prejudice. Within this pluralistic, multicultural society where the term *belief* has been usurped by fundamentalists of all brands to mean something concrete, as an alternative epistemology to natural science, how can I provide an answer when the term *belief* has lost its meaning? Can my understanding of belief really be conveyed to others? For example, as a Jew, does a belief in God signify God's existence or something else? We all know what Maimonides said about the statement "God exists."[1] Am I required to believe anything at all? As a self-defined secular Jew, have I in some way moved beyond these questions entirely? Put succinctly, no. Similar to the angst of the mercurial nineteenth-century German philosopher and poet Friedrich Nietzsche, I concede that any attempt to conceptualize a way beyond our world of philosophical and theological systems of thought and language by using precisely both is absurd. I challenge unceasingly both the heritage of Jewish tradition as well as modern culture and society. I belong to both and yet, paradoxically, I refuse to adduce reasons in support of overcoming either. I am trapped. On the one hand, I am wary of all traditions; on the other hand, I recognize the notion of "moving beyond" or "overcoming" them belongs with both schemas of thought and a fortiori must be met with the same suspicion. What, then, *can* I really believe without lapsing into the fire or the snow?

I recognize that my struggle perhaps characterizes a theological non-theology, though not what the German-Jewish thinker Franz Rosenzweig acerbically termed an *atheistic theology*. Jewish theology, for me, merely recognizes a wager. By accepting a priori that there is indeed meaning in meaning, I am making a wager on transcendence. I fully recognize and accept the arguments of those who assert that any comprehensible attempt to delineate or define language and how it operates, that our ability to convey thought, meaning, and emotion, by necessity infers transcendence. That the potential of language, more specifically of grammar, engenders our world is, I agree, the modus operandi of theological assumptions. Certainly these assumptions govern my own worldview, though the question is, do I believe them? I don't know—maybe, as Rosenzweig would say, "not yet"—though they certainly characterize and govern my life as a Jew. One could argue that this theological struggle is similar to the point Gershom Scholem made in his 1930 eulogy celebrating the life and thought of Rosenzweig, that Jewish theology is neither systematic nor is it a reflection on divine essence. It remains grounded in human questions. So, the performance of language, that is to say, our ability to communicate to some measure with one another, is in some sense the handmaiden to Jewish theology.

Rather than regard Jewish tradition, Jewish theology, and divinity— as some fundamental truth—as objects of stability and permanence, each as either the fire or the snow, I interpret them as inspired by the works of Rosenzweig and Martin Buber, as "events" that are always in the process of being rewritten, reinterpreted, and re-created. I experience Judaism (or possibly God), then, as an event, though I recognize the impossibility of acquiring this experience as knowledge and/or tradition, as an object to be imparted to others. It is more complicated. In the Torah, after Jacob ascends a stairway to heaven to encounter God, he awakens to say, "Surely the Lord is present in this place, and I did not know it!" (Genesis 28:16). As a result, he took the stone he used as a pillow and anointed it and renamed the place Bethel—"house of God" (Genesis 28:19). He transformed his experience into something he could pass on. He fashioned it, as Buber would say, as an "I-it" relationship. The second he took control of this experience (by placing a rock on the spot), the ever-present, ever-changing dialogue between him and God ceased. For Buber, the "I-thou" relationship—where one addresses the irreducible otherness of people or God—is a spontaneous, non-contrived meeting between people and other people, or between people and the ineffable Being, what we call God. Our experience of God is simply not something we can control. Jewish theology, for me, then, does not explain the world or God, but rather merely describes our relationship to both. So just as science and philosophy are progressive fields of knowledge that refine their assumptions when older ones are trumped by empirical data, belief, too, is an asymptotic activity that requires it to become more reasonable with each generation's evolving *Zeitgeist*. This keeps dialogue and the tradition alive. In this vein, Jewish tradition is a dynamic reaffirmation of itself: it is never static, and its goals and needs change with each generation that accepts and interprets it. It needs us as much as we need it to ensure that neither perishes into the fire or the snow.

Jewish tradition provides countless examples of this point. For instance, the school of Rabbi Ishmael made famous the teaching that the Torah is written in the language of human speech, yet this does not in any way compromise the divine quality of the Torah as divine speech. By accepting the divinity of the text a priori, within Rabbi Ishmael's thirteen hermeneutical principles, there is the insistence on multi-layered meaning, exoteric and esoteric interpretation, as well as the assumption that the Torah's accessibility affords us the opportunity to engage in dialogue within the text. For example, in the Torah the Deutoronimist writes, "Moses undertook to expound this teaching" (Deuteronomy 1:5). Extraordinary! Within our very canon this process of change is recorded, indeed canonized. Moses expounded the law within the law. Is his interpretation of the law more important than the law he is interpreting? What do we pass on? Again, to treat the Jewish experience as truth is to convert it into an object ("it"). By believing that God's word is something that can be objectified and passed from one person to the next, one generation to the next—as the essence of our tradition or of God's word—is to confound the proleptic character of God's word as an event that befalls each unique interpretative moment and encounter, which, of course, affords "every river [to have] its course" (BT *Chullin* 18b) God manifests this point in God's laconic reply to Moses during the scene of the burning bush that "*Ehyeh-Asher-Ehyeh*" (Exodus 3:14). Moreover this concept is within the Hebrew Bible itself.

This theological struggle informs my reading of all texts, sacred and profane, my experience of the world, and my experience of people. The Talmud still canonized the teachings of Elisha ben Abuyah, known as the *Acher*, the "other." Who today would deny that Jewish experience is replete with feelings of otherness—to ourselves, to others, to the world? All the more so, wouldn't these feelings of otherness translate to our experience of divinity? Gotthold Ephraim Lessing—the Enlightenment sage, playwright, theologian, and dear friend to Moses Mendelssohn and perhaps to all German-speaking Jews—once remarked that if presented with the choice between knowledge of absolute truth and the eternal quest for it, he would prefer the latter, since the former is for God alone. Though, Lessing's claim is too strong for me, I would argue, similarly, that the task of Jewish theology is to interpret, decipher, and communicate meaning, as opposed to "knowing" it. Interpretation for Jews is entirely a lived event. As a result, Jews must live between languages, cultures, and generations. Because each language speaks and constructs the world according to its own grammar, each language fashions and, indeed, circumscribes its own reality. Jews always live in the world in between the language of Judaism and their spoken language, so in some ways we are freer. To believe in the God of our forefathers and mothers is not to believe God exists, but rather to believe *in* God like I believe *in* feminism or *in* Judaism as ways to perceive and ameliorate our social environment, which of course, always changes.

Even though there are, in my opinion, limits to Jewish belief, Jewish continuity is in some sense a break from the previous generation. By allowing tradition to inform my life and vice versa, we both change. A dialogue with Judaism (or, more importantly, with God) is not a radical break with it, though it can lead to uncomfortable questions. It functions similarly to the acquisition and employment of language. For example, language contains in its basic structure a cultural presupposition from which all speech acts are created and repeated. No sentence is spoken *ex nihilo*, since already embedded in its grammar is a fixed worldview that confines all speech acts in a defined system. Writing is thus secondary because interpretation begins with speech. It is difficult to accept that the acquisition of language is random, since most respond to it as an inheritance that we are inescapably responsible for passing down through the generations. Language is a common property, and how we employ it is crucial to preserving or corrupting this inheritance. By understanding our relationship to God's word in this way, God's sentences do not change but our relationship to them does every moment we read them. Experience is not static. So to impose an ontology onto the text for me exceeds the bounds of Jewish interpretation and thought. We do not possess truth and read that backwards, otherwise how would we grow? Therein, I believe, lies our contemporary religious crisis. Since I agree with the neo-Kantian Jewish philosopher Hermann Cohen that Judaism is forward thinking, within our new postmodern universe we run into the problem of thinking *beyond* Judaism. Nonetheless, because I believe Judaism is best understood as a language, I recognize that I cannot move beyond it. For instance, Jewish tradition guards against the enunciation of the divine name, since once spoken, it lapses into indeterminacy and endless linguistic possibilities—meaning without meaning. As a result, God remains in *galut* (exile), since there is no absolute meaningful place for God to reside. As a Jew, I too, remain in this exile—not beyond the world, but rather, as mentioned above, stuck in between it.

This place in between is where Jewish theology takes place. Belief, here, of course, plays a different role. It is indeed a balancing act, which requires new questions. The new atheism advanced by Richard Dawkins and Christopher Hitchens provides some opportunity, though they are not necessarily compelling thinkers of religion in general, so their challenges still need to be met with some suspicion. I wonder how it is possible to argue "God is dead," since my experience, which is clearly postmodern, calls into question everything—including belief in God—to avert withering away in the fire or the snow. I am not interested in replacing one value—God—with another—us. According to Dawkins and Hitchens, religion provides an antiquated, irresponsible, and misconstrued explanation of the world. They prefer to offer a conflicting one. As I explained above, they are engaging in a different argument. Within their intransigent, atheistic universe, empirical science replaces theological inquiry. I would argue that there is no Archemedean point beyond the realm of universal equivalence; we are always stuck in between. As a result, authenticity, whether clothed in fundamentalist rants or in somber atheistic empiricism, is a façade. Every aspect of the world, whether theological or scientific, must be reevaluated or reinterpreted in order to maintain its being. Replacing one value with another (as Creationists, Dawkins, and Hitchens do, respectively) is not the task of Jewish theology, since it requires both sets of values. The fact that the new atheists challenge the very grounds for theology in general simply provides Jewish theology fertile ground to work in particular. In fact, Jewish atheists now have a voice within Judaism. For me, Jewish theology, unlike for fundamentalists or for Hitchens and Dawkins, inquires into why we even ask for explanations at all, and why we even consider a world where explanation is possible.

"Ben Zoma said: Who is wise? He who learns from everyone, as it is said, 'Because everyone has been my teacher, I have gained understanding' (Psalm 119:99)" (*Pirkei Avot* 4:1). Learning requires at least as much listening as it does speaking. An authentic teaching or conversation can take place only after you translate the speech of the other into your own. Jewish theology, as mentioned above, is precisely this translation. "All words of Torah need one another, for what one word closes, another opens" (*Midrash Tanchuma, Chukkot* 52). The theological dialectic between competing worldviews and translating between them is an ever-present and continuing process. Even though Sinai has also been at the center of Jewish theology, *galut* is not geographical. Otherness—*galut*—is precisely how Jews navigate the myriad spaces between realities. "For my plans are not your plans, nor my ways your ways, declares the Lord" (Isaiah 55:8). Ours is to always remain in between.

First Fruits of the Seasons of Hope and Renewal

RABBI NAAMAH KELMAN

When you enter the Land that Adonai your God is giving you
as a heritage…

—DEUTERONOMY 26:1

BRINGING THE FIRST FRUITS is a concise history of the essential biblical story, past, present, and future. It is also one of the only times where an individual Israelite offers a liturgy, a sacred declaration. One might call it a prototype for prayer. In eleven concise verses, a story unfolds before us. We imagine the Israelite farmer bearing his finest fruits to the holy site designated by God (later to become Jerusalem) where a priest awaits. A close reading of the verses does not really specify, so it might even be at the corner of a farmer's field where an itinerant priest is ever ready for the tithe. The place and the priest are less important. The centerpiece of this story is the story. We are our evolving story, and God is

---

Rabbi Naamah Kelman is dean of Hebrew Union College–Jewish Institute of Religion in Jerusalem. Born and raised in New York City, she has lived in Israel for over three decades. She is active in feminist causes and a staunch advocate of a Progressive, pluralistic, democratic Israel.

our guiding light—the beginning, middle, and end of each story, whether we tell it that way or not.

Deuteronomy 26 retells creation, exodus, and redemption wrapped up in a seemingly minor ritual practice. Yet closer examination of this text uncovers the enduring power of its multiple meanings reaching across the generations. Before the recitation of the *Sh'ma* became the centerpiece of almost every *t'fillah* (prayer), and with that the uncontested watchwords of our faith, the anthem of our people, the verses of Deuteronomy 26:5–8 were the most memorized of our emerging liturgy. These were the words recited by the farmer upon handing his first fruits over the priest. They were recited over the centuries at the Temple when the fruits were brought there. We know this from tractate *Bikkurim*. There, we are given a vivid description of the pageantry that evolved from the simple one-man ritual of the Bible to a full-blown majestic parade in the streets of Jerusalem, culminating with the king's reenactment of the ancient rite.

Because of the popularity of these words and, of course, their content, they found their way into the main section of the Passover Hagaddah. They are the key verses of the *Maggid* section, taken out of context and parsed into phrases with the accompanying midrash. Many readers do not really know their origin or their original purpose. These words remain a living, breathing story passed from one generation to the next at the Seder.

These verses and the full introduction and coda represent a theology of abundance. This is not something we usually internalize. We focus on the hardships and do not embrace the whole. Of course with the joy of abundance comes the obligation of responsibility. This is what is so startling about these verses. They capture the ongoing saga of creation and renewal and at the same time direct the individual to find the daily balance of mediating the broken and the whole. Our God is a God of justice, a God who intervenes in history. Our God is also a presence in our daily lives if we would just tell the story, keep to the story. And here is the full version of the story:

¹When you have come into the land which Adonai, your God, is giving you as a heritage, and have occupied it and settled in it, ²you shall take some first fruits of the various products of the soil which you harvest from the land which the Adonai, your God, gives you, and putting them in a basket, you shall go to the place which Adonai, your God, chooses for the dwelling place of God's name.

³There you shall go to the priest in office at that time and say to him, "Today I acknowledge Adonai, my God, that I have indeed come into the land which God swore to our fathers to give to us." ⁴The priest shall then receive the basket from you and shall set it in front of the altar of Adonai, your God. ⁵Then you shall declare before Adonai, your God, *"My father was a wandering Aramean who went down to Egypt with a small household and lived there as strangers. But there he became a nation great, strong, and numerous. ⁶When the Egyptians maltreated and oppressed us, imposing hard labor upon us, ⁷we cried to Adonai, the God of our fathers, and Adonai heard our cry and saw our affliction, our toil and our oppression. ⁸God brought us out of Egypt with a strong hand and outstretched arm, with terrifying power, with signs and wonders;* ⁹and bringing us into this country, God gave us this land flowing with milk and honey. ¹⁰Therefore, I have now brought you the first fruits of the products of the soil which you, O Adonai, have given me." And having set them before Adonai, your God, you shall bow down in God's presence. ¹¹Then you and your family, together with the Levite and the strangers who live among you, shall rejoice over all these good things which Adonai, your God, has given you.

The verses in italic are the verses that have been recited throughout the centuries at the Passover Seder, albeit not as a fluid narrative. The verses preceding this declaration take us back to the first time we entered the land but in actuality refer to each season's harvest and its first fruits. The land is given as a trust, because God has given it to the Israelites. It comes with certain conditions. These conditions include first and foremost a social welfare system that supports the clergy (priests and Levites), the poor and the stranger. When reciting our foundational and covenantal story of our oppression in Egypt, where we were enslaved strangers, we immediately translate this into action. The land is not for despoiling, for greedy consumption, for oppression.

Our Sages tell us that the first fruits are limited to the seven species, described earlier in Deuteronomy 8:8:

> A land of wheat and barley, of [grape] vines, figs and pomegranates, land of olive trees and honey.

Seven remains that mystical number denoting the seventh day as well. These fruits are the basics of daily consumption, native to the land dependent on the vagaries of weather and water supply. The Mishnah tells us that farmers living close to Jerusalem could bring fresh fruit while those coming from a distance could bring dried fruit. In coming to Jerusalem with fresh or dried fruits, we come to celebrate the "fruits of our labor." We come to share with those who do not have.

This rite was lost over the generations. Once the Temple was destroyed we no longer could bring the first fruits or any other sacrifice or offering of thanksgiving to the sacred site. These rites were transmuted into prayer and study and a wandering Jewish People. And yet, the kernel of this theology of abundance can be found in our prayer books, in our layers of interpretation of Torah, in our holidays. Of course, the short-hand rendition of the Exodus remained.

Why should any of this speak to us today? Might there be a theology here that makes sense in this postmodern world? Can we extract something for a modern State of Israel struggling with the challenges of sovereignty and a Diaspora living, for the most part, in security and comfort?

A theology of abundance is counter to affluence. A theology of gratitude is a reminder that we are vessels of God's gifts, not totally in control. A sense of abundance comes from bringing our first fruits. The word *reishit* in Hebrew can mean "first" and it can also mean "choicest." The word *bikkurim* comes later and is associated more closely with "firsts." *Reishit* is our best effort and our choicest produce. This is a spiritual practice of abundance.

Once there is abundance we can be generous. We reach out to the other, we feed the stranger. This is a commandment to share. Today's Israel struggles to share. The scarcity of resources, the fight for the same land, and the burdens of war and terror do not engender a sense of abundance. And yet, limited resources, a passion to survive and, indeed, to thrive, do cultivate creativity and generosity of spirit.

The Chasidic master Sefat Emet (Rabbi Yehuda Leib Alter), writing from Poland at the turn of the twentieth century, understood the significance of *reishit*. In his interpretation of Deutoronomy 26, he first quotes the Sages: "first fruits" would end with the destruction of the Temple, but instead, even Moses knew that they would be replaced by prayer. Our task each day is to make prayer become an act of bringing our *best* selves. By embracing creation every day, we can transform prayer and ourselves.

This eternal optimism is a challenge. Yet our sacred texts and prayers ground us in the cycle of creation-exodus-redemption. In our darkest hours, this gives us hope. In our strongest moments, this should give us pause.

AFTERWORD

RABBI ELLIOT J. COSGROVE, PhD

> The new currents in religious thought which we have
> examined are neither necessarily new nor necessarily
> confluent. They just happen to be the currents which are
> flowing at present. The fact that they flow in itself does
> not compel them to flow in harmony; yet we have sought
> through these essays to locate the common undertow
> which drags and pulls these currents into unity.
>
> MILTON STEINBERG, "NEW CURRENTS
> IN RELIGIOUS THOUGHT"[1]

Theology, it would seem, evolves. Both within each of us and across the
generations, what we can and do believe about God reflects a dynamic
process of clarification, revision, formulation, and testimony. This
anthology, embodying that process, provides a snapshot of the field,
filled with the hope that it will generate a dialogue among its readers.
Each author has spoken in his or her own voice toward constructing a
personal and passion-filled statement of Jewish belief. Their courage of
conviction and gifts of expression will hopefully serve as a springboard
for contemporary Jews seeking to develop their own theological voices.
Even where the reader identifies points of sharp difference, I hope this
volume provides a tool by which a questing Jew may refine his or her
own beliefs. As the prominent Jewish-American scholar Rabbi Arthur

Hertzberg once wrote: "One cannot affirm one's own certainties without understanding the counter-certainties of others."[2]

In reading and rereading the essays contained in this volume, you may find yourself (as I was) struck by an odd sense of variety and unity. Altogether remarkable is the lack of any single event or topic to which this cadre of new voices responds. There is no central pivot such as the Enlightenment, Shoah, or establishment of the State of Israel around which they revolve. There is no single Jewish or non-Jewish theologian with whom they all exist in dialogue, no "Death of God" challenge with which they all contend. The new atheists, though occupying much space in popular bookstores, do not appear to occupy these authors' concerns. Denominational identity does not shape the organization of the volume. Even their stylistic approaches vary from deeply personal testimony, to academic reflection, to neo-midrashic essays.

So what does this school of theologians represent, if anything at all? Are there common themes in their efforts?

Most identifiable is the inescapable universalism within these essays. They are "post-chosen" theologians in the sense that they are, for the most part, not driven by the task of negotiating the tension of wrought by being part of a "chosen people." Such anxiety is passé. In a pluralistic and multicultural world, it seems that chosenness is dead. In fact, it appears to be an a priori assumption of these thinkers that Judaism is but one of many, equally valid, options. We are all children of a common God. As Rabbi Or Rose states in his contribution, "I do not believe that the Jewish People are God's chosen people and I do not consider Judaism superior to other religions." With very few exceptions, the lack of mention of Israel, Jewish peoplehood, and other markers of Jewish particularism—theological, national, cultural, or otherwise—serve as notable data points shared among these thinkers. While Jewish, these theologians are not parochial, in that they insist on existing side by side with other faith traditions and with our common humanity, and addressing the shared concerns of the universal condition.

There is also a democratic, if not populist, feel to these contributions. One would never guess from this volume that Jewish theology has traditionally been a somewhat elite enterprise, conducted by a select few under specific interpretive parameters, and authorized by tightly controlled rabbinic sanction. Here, it would seem, "Catholic Israel" has been supplanted by a "Protestant Israel" in that every Jew may now interpret sacred texts on his or her own authority. Jewish theology has been elevated or reduced (depending on your point of view) to being the creative result of a Jew finding meaning in a text. Biblical, rabbinic, Chasidic, and contemporary texts stand equally in this system. If a text is bothersome, it can be ignored; if it forwards your theological view, it is authoritative. More startling is the emergence of the text of the "self," namely the notion that a Jew's own life experiences are, unto themselves, the stuff of Jewish theology. Such a state of affairs raises all sorts of questions: May I use the thought of a non-Jew toward constructing my Jewish theology? If so, who draws the line between using Emerson and Montaigne as opposed to the Bhagavdad Gita? Are my questions, joys, failures, and agonies "Jewish" by dint of me being a Jew, or do they only become Jewish when read through a Jewish text? Alternatively, is Jewish theology only valid if I am able to appropriate the insights of an authorized rabbinic predecessor to speak to my modern condition?

To be fair, such questions are not necessarily new to this book. Nevertheless, in this time of the flattening of authority structures, we must be ever mindful of the challenges brought by the freedoms of our age.

Despite our best efforts, there are imbalances in this anthology. The lack of Orthodox voices, though not by choice, has resulted in a volume predominated by Jews of a liberal inflection. Personal autonomy is a given. Even those purporting to feel the weight of God on their shoulders are aware that it is a willed choice. The texts we choose to interpret, the observance patterns we follow, are choices, opportunities to strive toward God and discern the divine will. On this count, it seems that the authors are struggling to find the language by which to capture a sense of being radically free and radically claimed, as described by Rabbi Rachel Sabbath Beit-Halachmi, or trying to see Jewish observance as a "vow freely made," as described by Rabbi Michael Marmur. Perhaps more than anything else, it is this effort to validate the autonomous Jewish self and retain a binding theological sensibility that is the common denominator shared among these authors. I, for one, would love to see an anthology of Orthodox voices who, while aware of the claims of modernity, do not understand their beliefs and observances as a willed choice.

Finally, and perhaps underlying it all, is the theological humility embedded within these chapters. A far cry from Maimonides' unflinching principles of faith, these authors (myself included) are less assertive. Statements of belief are framed tentatively, ever anticipating the counterclaims of others, not to mention those held by the author. As Benjamin Sax noted with Woody Allen's famous quip, "I am Jewish, but with an explanation."

We are hardly the first generation of theologians to write theology filled with hesitation. One could argue that all theological thought, certainly since the Enlightenment, has had a *"yes ... but ..."* quality to it. What is the modern Jewish condition if not the task of affirming belief (*"yes"*), all the while acknowledging the very challenges posed by holding those beliefs (*"but"*)? Certainly in an age of fundamentalism a little bit of doubt goes a long way. Nevertheless, liberal theologians need to regain and retain their nerve. God cannot be let to die by way of a thousand qualifications. We need to be filled with theological gumption, able to make positive statements of belief, both convinced and convincing, all the while respectful of others and the divine mystery around us all.

Deeply creative, universal in orientation, fiercely democratic, proudly autonomous, and suffused by a deep humility—these are the attributes of our collective theologians. Whether these traits are strengths or weaknesses, only the reader and time will tell. May these essays prod us forward on our theological journeys.

NOTES

Introduction

1. Mordecai Kaplan, *Judaism as a Civilization: Towards a Reconstruction of American Jewish Life* (Philadelphia: Jewish Publication Society, 1934), 393–394.
2. Arthur Hertzberg, *The Jews in America: Four Centuries of an Uneasy Encounter—A History* (New York: Columbia University Press, 1997), 374.
3. Joseph Albo, *Sefer Ha-Ikkarim*, II, 30, ed. Husik, 206.
4. Solomon Schechter, "The Dogmas in Judaism," in Solomon Schechter, *Studies in Judaism: First Series* (Philadelphia: Jewish Publication Society, 1911), 104.
5. Louis Jacobs, "Montefiore and Loewe on the Rabbis," in Louis Jacobs, *Rabbinic Thought in the Talmud* (Edgeware: Vallentine Mitchell, 2005), 130–131.
6. Byron Sherwin, "An Incessantly Gushing Fountain: The Nature of Jewish Theology," in *Contemporary Jewish Theology: A Reader*, ed. Elliot N. Dorff and Louis E. Newman (New York: Oxford University Press, 1999), 7ff.

I Will Be Who I Will Be: A God of Dynamic Becoming by Rabbi Bradley Shavit Artson, DHL

1. "Almighty," found in English translations, is not a biblical or rabbinic phrase. The King James Bible used this term to translate the Hebrew *shaddai*. But *shaddai* does not mean all-powerful. Scholars tell us that *shaddai* derives from a term for mountains. So *el shaddai* is the God of the mountains, and it is also possibly related to the word *shadayim*, which means "breasts."

Living and Dreaming with God by Rabbi Shai Held

1. Maimonides, *Guide of the Perplexed*, III:53 (Pines translation).
2. The paragraphs in this section are reproduced (with some minor changes) from my essay "*Hadesh Yamenu*," *Judaism* 54 no. 3–4 (Summer/Fall 2005): 165–173. I am grateful to the editors of *Judaism* for permission to use this material.
3. Cf. JT *N'darim* 9:7, *Mishnah Sanhedrin* 4:5, and *Mishnah Avot* 3:14.
4. Cf. Rabbi Abraham Isaac Kook, "*Chakham Adif MiNavi*," in *Orot* (Hebrew) (Jerusalem: Mossad Harav Kook, 1963), 120–121. A useful English translation appears in Michael Walzer, et al., eds., *The Jewish Political Tradition: Authority* (New Haven: Yale University Press, 2000), 271–273.
5. Cf. Abraham Joshua Heschel, *God in Search of Man* (New York: Farrar, Straus, and Giroux, 1955), 323, 338–346.
6. Cf., for starters, *Sifrei Deuteronomy* 49; BT *Sotah* 14a; and Maimonides, *Guide of the Perplexed*, 1:54, 3:54, and esp. 3:53.
7. Cf. Leviticus 19:33–34 and Exodus 23:9.

8. The careful reader will note: where walking in God's ways is concerned, covenant reinforces and deepens what is already implicit in creation, namely the mandate to become like God.

9. The exact meaning of *venivrekhu v'kha kol mishp'chot ha'adamah* (Genesis 12:3) is not entirely clear. Scholars disagree about whether the phrase means that "all the families of the earth shall be blessed through you" or, rather, that "all the families of the earth shall bless themselves by you." A consideration of this question is obviously far beyond the scope of this essay. A useful discussion by a contemporary Christian scholar can be found in R.W.L. Moberly, *The Theology of the Book of Genesis* (Cambridge: Cambridge, 2009), 141–161.

Non-dual Judaism by Rabbi James Jacobson-Maisels

1. Rabbi Jacob Joseph of Polonne, *Ben Porat Yosef*, 94a, 339–40.

2. See Rabbi Shneur Zalman of Liadi, *Tanya, Shaar Yichud 'Emunah*, chapt. 1.

3. Negative theology is the claim that due to God's transcendence of all attributions and characteristics, the only acceptable way to refer to God's qualities or nature is through negative statements such as "God is not limited." Panentheism is the claim that everything (the entire cosmos) is God (radical immanence) but unlike pantheism, that God is also beyond the cosmos (transcendence).

4. As Rabbi Isaac of Acre taught, "She [the soul] will cleave to divine intellect, and it will cleave to her ... and she and intellect become one entity, as if somebody pours out a jug of water into a running well, that all becomes one." *Ozar Hayyim*, MS Moscow-Gunzberg 775, fol. 111a. trans. Moshe Idel, *Kabbalah: New Perspectives*, 67.

5. See, for instance, *Maggid D'varav L'Yaakov* 78, p. 134.

6. Rabbi Jacob Joseph of Polonne, *Ben Porat Yosef*, 94a, pp. 339–40, quoting *Genesis Rabbah* (Vilna) 21:5.

7. Paralleling the *sefirot* of *Keter, Chokhmah, Binah, Chesed, G'vurah, Tiferet, Netzach, Hod, Y'sod*, and *Malkhut*.

8. Rabbi Azriel of Gerona, *Path of Faith and Path of Heresy*, in Gershom Scholem, *New Fragments from the Writings of Rabbi Azriel of Gerona: Studies in Memory of Asher Gulak and Samuel Klein*, ed. Simhah Assaf and Gershom Scholem (Jerusalem: Hebrew University, 1942), 207.

9. *Meor Eynayim, hashmatot, re'eh, d"h ketiv aharei h' telekhu*, pp. 240–241.

10. See Gershom Scholem, *"Sitra Ahra*: Good and Evil in the Kabbalah," in *On the Mystical Shape of the Godhead* (New York: Schocken, 1997), 56–72; and the teaching of Ezra of Gerona there; Eitan Fishbane, *Contemplative Practice and the Transmission of Kabbalah: A Study of Isaac of Acre's Me'irat 'Einayim* (Boston: Brandeis PhD diss., 2003), 262.

11. As in the *p'shat* understanding of the *Aleinu* prayer above.

12. This term is taken from Tara Brach and her book *Radical Acceptance: Embracing Your Life with the Heart of a Buddha* (New York: Bantam, 2004). See my article "Inviting the Demons In: A Hasidic Approach to Suffering, Conflict and Human Failings," in *Kerem* 11 (5768/2007–2008), for a deeper exploration of this question.

13. Rabbi Dov Baer the Maggid of Mezritch, *Maggid D'varav L'Yaakov*, 29, p. 48.

14. *Keter Shem Tov*, 75, 87c. By resisting our suffering we add insult to injury, adding psychological stress, tensions, fear, anger, and a host of other difficult emotions to the bare experience of pain.

Notes

15. See Elijah de Vidas, *Reishit Chokhmah, Sha'ar ha-Anavah.*
16. *Maggid D'varav L'Yaakov* 200, p. 325.
17. Rabbi Moshe Hayim Ephraim of Sudylkow, *Degel Mahaneh Ephraim, Bereshit Barah Elohim,* p. 1; *Sefat Emet, Ki Tavo,* 5632, *d"h bamidrash im shamoa, Esh Kodesh Yitro* 5702.
18. Rabbi Menahem Nahum of Chernobyl, *Meor Eynayim, Likutim, d"h tov li torat pikha,* pp. 284–285.
19. Rabbi Naphtali Zevi of Ropshitz, *Zera Kodesh, Shavuot,* p. 40a, Jerusalem, 5731.
20. For silence as *ayin,* see *Likutei Moharan* 64.
21. See Gershom Scholem, "The Meaning of the Torah in Jewish Mysticism," in *On the Kabbalah and Its Symbolism* (New York: Schocken Books, 1996), 66–86; Moshe Idel, *Absorbing Perfections* (New Haven: Yale University Press, 2002), 59ff.
22. Rabbi Moshe Hayyim Ephraim of Sudylkow, *Degel Mahaneh Ephraim, Re'eh, Od yirmoz ki yadua anokhi,* p. 224.
23. Moses, whom I understand not (only) as a historical being, but as the mythic representation of the primordial revelation of our people.
24. Rabbi Yehuda Leib Alter of Ger, *Sefat Emet, Ki Teitzei,* 5660.
25. For instance, Rabbi Mordecai Joseph Leiner of Izbica, *Mei Hashiloach, VaYigash,* vol. 1, *vayomer Yisrael.*
26. *Maggid D'varav L'Yaakov* 77, pp. 132–133. It is in this way that the patriarchs, as the midrash describes, performed *mitzvot* even before Torah was given. Their actions, too, aimed at the same underlying transformation of consciousness.
27. *Guide of the Perplexed* III:51.
28. Rabbi Levi Yitzhak of Berdichev, *K'dushat Levi* (Jerusalem: *Mosad l'hotzaot sifrei musar v'hasidut,* 1958), 33.
29. *Sefat Emet, Ki Teitzei,* 5660.
30. In this case, submission to the yolk of heaven.
31. *Mei Hashiloach,* I, Noah, Vienna 1860, 5b.

A Progressive Reform Judaism by Rabbi Evan Moffic
1. Jonathan Sacks, *The Dignity of Difference* (New York: Continuum, 2002), 55.

Spiritual Mappings: A Jewish Understanding of Religious Diversity by Rabbi Or N. Rose
1. Eleazar of Worms, *Sefer ha-Shem;* see Daniel C. Matt, *The Essential Kabbalah: The Heart of Jewish Mysticism* (New York: HarperCollins, 1996), 25, 166.
2. Abraham Joshua Heschel, *God in Search of Man* (Philadelphia: Jewish Publication Society, 1956), 185.
3. John D. Levenson, "The Universal Horizon of Biblical Particularism," in *Ethnicity and the Bible,* edited by Mark G. Brett (Boston: Brill, 2002), 145.
4. David Stern, "Midrash and Jewish Interpretation," in *The Jewish Study Bible,* edited by Adele Berlin and Marc Zvi Brettler (New York: Oxford University Press, 2004), 1863.
5. Abraham Joshua Heschel, "No Religion Is an Island," in *Moral Grandeur and Spiritual Audacity: Essays,* edited by Susannah Heschel (New York: Farrar, Straus, and Giroux, 1997), 237.
6. Ibid.

Five Pillars of Orthodox Judaism by Rabbi Asher

1. Joel Roth, *Homosexuality Revisited* (Rabbinical Assembly, 2006).
2. Cf. *Nefesh Hachayim*, Rav Chayim Volozner, Gate 4, Ch. 11.

Martin Buber: The Dialogue with God by Rabbi William Plevan

1. For further study on this topic, see Martin Buber's "The Holy Way" and "The Dialogue Between Heaven and Earth" in *On Judaism* (New York: Schocken, 1967) and "The Faith of Israel" and "Two Foci of the Jewish Soul" in *Israel and the World: Essays in a Time of Crisis* (Syracuse: Syracuse University Press, 1997).

Radically Free and Radically Claimed: Toward the Next Stage of Liberal Jewish Theology by Rabbi Rachel Sabath Beit-Halachmi, PhD

1. One Reform Movement expression of this stance is the 1999 CCAR Statement of Principles, available at: http://ccarnet.org/Articles/index.cfm?id=44&pge_prg_id=4687&pge_id=1656.
2. I use this term somewhat differently than does the Jewish French philosopher Emmanuel Levinas, but first encountered it as a foundational Jewish religious concept in Levinas' *Difficult Freedom* (Baltimore: Johns Hopkins University Press, 1990).
3. Eugene B. Borowitz, "The Autonomous Jewish Self," *Modern Judaism* 4, no. 1 (1984): 40–56; and *Renewing the Covenant: A Theology for the Postmodern Jew* (Philadelphia: Jewish Publication Society, 1991).
4. Use of the terms *radically free* and *radically claimed* both here and in the title of this chapter are intentional responses to the covenant theologies of David Hartman, a modern Orthodox rabbi and scholar; and of Eugene B. Borowitz, a leading liberal rabbi, scholar, and theologian. Hartman argues specifically for a Jewish self that is both "radically claimed and radically free." This chapter takes as its premise that liberal Jews know themselves to be radically free, and yet are also radically claimed.
5. Walter Jacob, "'The Law of the Lord Is Perfect': Halakhah and Antinomism in Reform Judaism," *CCAR Journal* 51, no. 3 (2004): 72–84.
6. The term is based on a Greek myth. It means that we are "like dwarfs on the shoulders of giants," so that we can see more than they, and things at a greater distance, not by virtue of any sharpness of sight on our part, or any physical distinction, but because we are carried high and raised up by their giant size.
7. Abraham Isaac Kook, *Ohrot HaKodesh* (*Lights of Holiness*) (Jerusalem: Mosad Harav Kook, 1985).
8. Franz Rosenzweig, "The Builders," in *On Jewish Learning* (Madison: University of Wisconsin, 2002).
9. The commitment to the Jewish People is not only about the survival of the Jewish People, in light of the Shoah, but its flourishing in affirmation of the historic opportunities of the reality of the Jewish State and an embrace of the unprecedented opportunity to live fully in partnership with non-Jews in the Diaspora, especially in North America.
10. David Hartman, "Judaism as an Interpretive Tradition," in *A Heart of Many Rooms: Celebrating the Many Voices within Judaism* (Woodstock, VT: Jewish Lights Publishing, 2001), 3ff.

11. All of my adult life I have been acutely aware of the ideological and theological implications at issue, given that at my bat mitzvah in a classical Reform synagogue I was coached to avoid saying "according to the Torah that God gave to us on Mt. Sinai" but rather "according to the Torah which God inspired on Mt. Sinai."
12. Eugene B. Borowitz, "On Celebrating Sinai," *CCAR Journal* 13, no. 6 (1966): 12–23. Reprinted in Borowitz, *Studies in the Meaning of Judaism* (Philadelphia: Jewish Publication Society, 2002).
13. *Bava Metzia* 59b: Rabbi Nathan met the prophet Elijah. He asked him, "What was the Holy One, Blessed be He, doing in that hour?" Said Elijah, "He was laughing and saying, 'My children have defeated me, my children have defeated me.'"
14. Hartman, 9.
15. Abraham Joshua Heschel, "The Meaning of this Hour," in *Moral Grandeur and Spiritual Audacity* (New York: Farrar, Straus, and Giroux, 1997).

A Quest-Driven Faith by Rabbi Elliot J. Cosgrove, PhD

1. I readily acknowledge my intellectual and spiritual debt to Louis Jacobs (1920–2006) and Abraham Joshua Heschel (1907–1972). While the language and mood of a quest as an authentic mode of Jewish theology did not originate with Jacobs or Heschel, it is through them that it gained its most articulate contemporary spokesmen. Theology must be personal but it need not be original, and my debt to Jacobs and Heschel is ongoing. In fact, if anything contained herein is worthy of expansion or in need of clarification or correction, then I recommend any of their books toward this goal.
2. William James, *The Varieties of Religious Experience* (New York: Penguin, 1985), 31.
3. Mordecai Kaplan, *A New Zionism* (New York: Theodor Herzl Foundation, 1955), 114.

Theological Proximity: The Quest for Intimacy with God by Simon Cooper, PhD

1. Joseph B. Soloveitchik, *The Lonely Man of Faith*, 2nd ed. (New York: Doubleday, 1992), 2.
2. Soloveitchik, 47.
3. Maimonides, *Guide for the Perplexed*, 3:51.
4. Maimonides championed fundamentals of the faith (*ikkarim* or *y'sodot*) not only in the Thirteen Principles of Faith, but also in chapter one of the *Guide for the Perplexed* and in the very first chapter of the *Mishneh Torah*, aptly named *Y'sodei HaTorah* (The Foundations of the Torah).
5. Julius Guttmann, *Philosophies of Judaism* (New York: Schocken, 1973), 3.

Longing to Hear Again by Rabbi Leon A. Morris

1. Paul Mendes-Flohr, *Divided Passions: Jewish Intellectuals and the Experience of Modernity* (Detroit: Wayne State University, 1991), 287–288
2. Elie Holzer, "The Concept of Second Naivete," in *Languages and Literatures in Jewish Education: Studies in Honor of Michael Rosenak* (Jerusalem: Magnes Press, 2007), 326
3. Paul Ricoeur, *The Symbolism of Evil* (Boston: Beacon, 1968), 351.
4. Ibid., 350–351.
5. Ibid., 351.

6. Hans Georg Gadamer, *Truth and Method* (New York: Continuum, 2004), 292.
7. This contrast is one I was introduced to in *The Burnt Book: Reading the Talmud*, trans. Marc-Alain Ouaknin (Princeton, NJ: Princeton University Press, 1995).
8. Holzer, 327–328.
9. I am grateful to Elie Holzer for highlighting for me the difficulties of applying the notion of second naivete to someone who had never fully experienced a first naivete grounded in traditional Jewish belief and practice.
10. Holzer, 329.

Walking the Walk by Rabbi Daniel Nevins

1. Robert M. Cover, "The Supreme Court, 1982—Forward: Nomos and Narrative," *Harvard Law Review* 97, no. 4 (1983).

On This Sacred Ground by Rabbi Eliyahu Stern

1. Chaim Grade, "My Quarrel with Hersh Rasseyner" in *A Treasury.of Yiddish Stories*, Irving Howe and Eliezer Greenberg, eds. (New York: Penguin, 1989).

The Radical Divinity by Rabbi Tamar Elad-Appelbaum

1. Eliezer Ashkenazi Ha-Rofe, *Sefer Ma'asei Hashem: Sha'ar Ma'aseh Torah, Parashat Balak* (Jerusalem: Merkaz Ha'Sefer, 2005), section 31, 369. I wish to thank Rabbi Michael Graetz for introducing me to this book as well as for his enlightening comments on this paper generally.
2. Avraham Yitzhak Hakohen Kook, *(Siddur) Olat Re'eyah*, Pt. I: p. 330. Cf. in his *'Eyn Ayah, B'rakhot* II.89, section 361.
3. Martin Buber, *Tales of the Hasidim: Later Masters.* (New York: Schocken, 1961), 145.
4. *Tzava'at ha-Ribash* (Jerusalem: Chorev, 1948), section 325, 14.

How I Came to Theology, or Didn't by Rabbi Daniel Bronstein, PhD

1. Linas Eli, ed., *Ohr Yisrael: The Classic Writings of Rav Yisrael Salanter and His Disciple Rav Yitzchak Blazer.* Zvi Miller, trans. (Southfield, MI: Targum/Feldheim, 2004), 358.
2. Ibid, 251.
3. Ibid, 279.

The Theology of the *In-Between* by Benjamin Sax, PhD

1. In *Guide of the Perplexed,* Maimonides writes, "All we understand is the fact that [God] exists, that [God] is a being to whom none of Adonai's creatures is similar, who has nothing in common with them, who does not include plurality, who is never too feeble to produce other beings and whose relation to the universe is that of a steersman to a boat; and even this is not a real relation, a real simile, but serves only to convey to us the idea that God rules the universe, that it is [God] that gives it duration and preserves its necessary arrangement."

Afterword by Rabbi Elliot J. Cosgrove, PhD

1. In Milton Steinberg, *Anatomy of Faith*, 1st ed. (New York: Harcourt, Brace, 1960), 299.
2. Arthur Hertzberg, *The Jews in America: Four Centuries of an Uneasy Encounter : A History* (New York: Columbia University Press, 1997), 459.

SUGGESTIONS FOR FURTHER READING

Adler, Rachel. *Engendering Judaism: An Inclusive Theology and Ethics*. Boston: Beacon Press, 1999.

Angel, Marc D. *Maimonides, Spinoza and Us: Toward an Intellectually Vibrant Judaism*. Woodstock, VT: Jewish Lights, 2009.

Baeck, Leo. *The Essence of Judaism*. Translated by Irving Howe and Victor Grubwieser. New York: Schocken Books, 1961.

Borowitz, Eugene B. *Choices in Modern Jewish Thought: A Partisan Guide*. Springfield, NJ: Behrman House, 1995.

———. *Liberal Judaism*. New York: URJ Press, 1984.

———. *Renewing the Covenant: A Theology for the Postmodern Jew*. Philadelphia: Jewish Publication Society, 1996.

———. *Studies in the Meaning of Judaism*. Philadelphia: Jewish Publication Society, 2002.

———. *A Touch of the Sacred: A Theologian's Informal Guide to Jewish Belief*. Woodstock, VT: Jewish Lights, 2009.

Buber, Martin. *I and Thou*. Translated by Walter Kaufman and S. G. Smith. New York: Charles Scribner, 1970.

———. *Israel and the World: Essays in a Time of Crisis*. Syracuse: Syracuse University Press, 1997.

———. *On Judaism*. New York: Schocken Books, 1996.

———. *Two Types of Faith*. Edited by Norman P. Goldhawk. Syracuse: Syracuse University Press, 2003.

———. *The Way of Response: Martin Buber—Selections from His Writings*. Edited by Nahum Glatzer. New York: Schocken Books, 1966.

Chesterton, G.K. *Orthodoxy*. Chicago: Moody Publishers, 2009.

Cohen, Arthur A. *Arguments and Doctrines: A Reader of Jewish Thinking in the Aftermath of the Holocaust*. New York: Harper and Row, 1970.

———. *The Natural and Supernatural Jew: An Historical and Theological Introduction*. 2nd edition. Springfield, NJ: Behrman House, 1979.

———. *The Tremendum: A Theological Interpretation of the Holocaust*. New York: Continuum, 1993.

Cohen, Arthur A., and Paul R. Mendes-Flohr, eds. *Contemporary Jewish Religious Thought: Original Essays on Critical Concepts, Movements, and Beliefs*. New York: Free Press, 1988.

Cohen, Steven M., and Arnold M. Eisen. *The Jew Within: Self, Family, and Community in America*. Bloomington: Indiana University Press, 2000.

Cohon, Samuel Solomon. *Jewish Theology: A Historical and Systematic Interpretation of Judaism and Its Foundations*. Assen: Van Gorcum, 1971.

Commentary. *Condition of Jewish Belief: A Symposium Compiled by the Editors of Commentary Magazine*. Northvale, NJ: Jason Aronson, 1995.

Dewey, John. *A Common Faith*. New Haven: Yale University Press, 1960.

Dorff, Elliot N. *Knowing God: Jewish Journeys to the Unknowable*. Northvale, NJ: Jason Aronson, 1996.

Dorff, Elliot N., and Louis E. Newman, eds. *Contemporary Jewish Theology: A Reader*. New York: Oxford University Press, 1998.

Eisen, Arnold M. *Taking Hold of Torah: Jewish Commitment and Community in America*. Bloomington: Indiana University Press, 2000.

Emerson, Ralph Waldo. *Essays: First and Second Series*. New York: Vintage, 1990.

Eskenazi, Tamara Cohn, and Andrea Weiss. *The Torah: A Women's Commentary*. New York: URJ Press, 2007.

Fackenheim, Emil L. *The Jewish Thought of Emil Fackenheim: A Reader*. Edited by Michael L. Morgan. Detroit: Wayne State University Press, 1987.

———. *Quest for Past and Future: Essays in Jewish Theology*. Boston: Beacon Press, 2000.

———. *To Mend the World: Foundations of Future Jewish Thought*. New York: Schocken Books, 1988.

Feinstein, Edward. *Jews and Judaism in the Twenty-first Century: Human Responsibility, the Presence of God, and the Future of the Covenant*. Woodstock, VT: Jewish Lights, 2008.

Fishbane, Michael A. *Sacred Attunement: A Jewish Theology*. Chicago: University of Chicago Press, 2008.

Gillman, Neil. *Doing Jewish Theology: God, Torah and Israel in Modern Judaism*. Woodstock, VT: Jewish Lights, 2010.

———. *Sacred Fragments: Recovering Theology for the Modern Jew*. Philadelphia: Jewish Publication Society, 1992.

———. *Traces of God: Seeing God in Torah, History, and Everyday Life*. Woodstock, VT: Jewish Lights, 2006.

———. *The Way Into Encountering God in Judaism*. Woodstock, VT: Jewish Lights, 2004.

Glatzer, Nahum Norbert. *Franz Rosenzweig: His Life and Thought*. 3rd ed. Indianapolis: Hackett, 1998.

Goldstein, Elyse, ed. *New Jewish Feminism: Probing the Past, Forging the Future*. Woodstock, VT: Jewish Lights, 2008.

———, ed. *The Women's Haftarah Commentary: New Insights from Women Rabbis on the 54 Weekly Haftarah Portions, the 5 Megillot and Special Shabbatot*. Woodstock, VT: Jewish Lights, 2008.

———, ed. *The Women's Torah Commentary: New Insights from Women Rabbis on the 54 Weekly Torah Portions*. Woodstock, VT: Jewish Lights, 2008.

Goldy, Robert G. *The Emergence of Jewish Theology in America*. Bloomington: Indiana University Press, 1990.

Green, Arthur. *Jewish Spirituality: From the Bible through the Middle Ages*. New York: Routledge, 1986.

———. *Jewish Spirituality: From the Sixteenth-Century Revival to the Present*. New York: Crossroad, 1989.

———. *Radical Judaism: Rethinking God and Tradition*. New Haven: Yale University Press, 2010.

———. *Seek My Face: A Jewish Mystical Theology*. Woodstock, VT: Jewish Lights, 2003.

Greenberg, Irving. *The Jewish Way: Living the Holidays*. Northvale, NJ: Jason Aronson, 1998.

Guttmann, Julius. *Philosophies of Judaism*. New York: Schocken Books, 1973.

Halivni, David. *Revelation Restored: Divine Writ and Critical Responses*. Boulder, CO: Westview Press, 1998.

Halivni, David, and Peter Ochs. *Breaking the Tablets: Jewish Theology after the Shoah*. Lanham: Rowman and Littlefield, 2007.

Hartman, David. *A Heart of Many Rooms: Celebrating the Many Voices within Judaism*. Woodstock, VT: Jewish Lights, 2001.

———. *Joy and Responsibility: Israel, Modernity and the Renewal of Judaism*. Jerusalem: Ben-Zvi-Posner, 1978.

———. *A Living Covenant: The Innovative Spirit in Traditional Judaism*. Woodstock, VT: Jewish Lights, 1998.

———. *Love and Terror in the God Encounter: The Theological Legacy of Rabbi Joseph B. Soloveitchik*. Woodstock, VT: Jewish Lights, 2004.

Hertzberg, Arthur. *The Jews in America*. New York: Columbia University Press, 1998.

Heschel, Abraham Joshua. *God in Search of Man: A Philosophy of Judaism*. New York: Farrar, Straus, and Giroux, 1976.

———. *Man's Quest for God: Studies in Prayer and Symbolism*. New York: Scribner, 1954.

———. *Man Is Not Alone: A Philosophy of Religion*. New York: Farrar, Straus, and Giroux, 1976.

———. *Moral Grandeur and Spiritual Audacity: Essays*. New York: Farrar, Straus, and Giroux, 1997.

———. *The Sabbath*. New York: Farrar, Straus, and Giroux, 2005.

Idel, Moshe. *Absorbing Perfections: Kabbalah and Interpretation*. New Haven: Yale University Press, 2002.

Jacobs, Louis. *Faith*. Eugene, OR: Wipf and Stock, 2008.

———. *God, Torah, Israel: Traditionalism without Fundamentalism*. Cincinnati: Hebrew Union College Press, 1990.

———. *A Jewish Theology*. Springfield, NJ: Behrman House, 1973.

———. *Principles of the Jewish Faith: An Analytical Study*. Eugene, OR: Wipf and Stock, 2008.

———. *Rabbinic Thought in the Talmud*. London: Vallentine Mitchell, 2005.

———. *We Have Reason to Believe: Some Aspects of Jewish Theology Examined in the Light of Modern Thought*. 5th ed. London: Vallentine Mitchell, 2004.

James, William. *Pragmatism and Other Writings*. Edited by Giles Gunn. New York: Penguin, 2002.

———. *The Varieties of Religious Experience*. New York: Library of America, 2009.

———. *The Will to Believe and Other Essays in Popular Philosophy*. Ann Arbor: University of Michigan Library, 2009.

Kadushin, Max. *The Rabbinic Mind*. New York: Jewish Theological Seminary of America, 1952.

Kaplan, Mordecai. *Judaism As a Civilization: Toward a Reconstruction of American-Jewish Life*. Philadelphia: Jewish Publication Society, 1994.

———. *The Meaning of God in Modern Jewish Religion*. Detroit: Wayne State University Press, 1994.

Kaufman, William E. *Contemporary Jewish Philosophies*. Detroit: Wayne State University Press, 1992.

Kellner, Menachem. *Must a Jew Believe Anything?* 2nd ed. London: Littman Library, 2006.

Kohler, K. *Jewish Theology: Systematically and Historically Considered*. Jersey City, NJ: KTAV, 1968.

Kushner, Harold S. *When Bad Things Happen to Good People*. New York: Anchor, 2004.

Leibowitz, Yeshayahu. *Accepting the Yoke of Heaven : Commentary on the Weekly Torah Portion*. Jerusalem: Urim Publications, 2006.

Levenson, Jon. *Sinai and Zion: An Entry into the Jewish Bible*. New York: HarperOne, 1987.

Levinas, Emmanuel. *Difficult Freedom: Essays on Judaism*. Baltimore: Johns Hopkins University Press, 1990.

Marty, Martin E. *Modern American Religion*. 3 vols. Chicago: University of Chicago Press, 1999.

Mendes-Flohr, Paul. *Divided Passions: Jewish Intellectuals and the Experience of Modernity*. Detroit: Wayne State University, 1991.

Mendes-Flohr, Paul R., and Jehuda Reinharz. *The Jew in the Modern World: A Documentary History*. 2nd ed. New York: Oxford University Press, 1995.

Muffs, Yochanan. *Love and Joy: Law, Language and Religion in Ancient Israel*. New York: Jewish Theological Seminary, 1995.

———. *The Personhood of God: Biblical Theology, Human Faith and the Divine Image*. Woodstock, VT: Jewish Lights, 2009.

Neusner, Jacob. *Understanding Jewish Theology: Classical Issues and Modern Perspectives*. Jersey City, NJ: KTAV, 1973.

Noll, Mark A. *America's God: From Jonathan Edwards to Abraham Lincoln*. New York: Oxford University Press, 2005.

Ochs, Peter. *The Return to Scripture in Judaism and Christianity: Essays in Postcritical Scriptural Interpretation*. Eugene, OR: Wipf and Stock, 2008.

Plaskow, Judith. *Standing Again at Sinai: Judaism from a Feminist Perspective*. New York: HarperOne, 1991.

Rosenzweig, Franz. *On Jewish Learning*. Madison: University of Wisconsin, 2002.

Rosenzweig, Franz. *The Star of Redemption*. Translated by Barbara E. Galli. Madison: University of Wisconsin Press, 2005.

Ross, Tamar. *Expanding the Palace of Torah: Orthodoxy and Feminism*. Hanover, NH: Brandeis University Press, 2004.

Rotenstreich, Nathan, and Paul R. Mendes-Flohr. *On Faith*. Chicago: University of Chicago Press, 1998.

Sacks, Jonathan. *The Dignity of Difference: How to Avoid the Clash of Civilizations*. New York: Continuum, 2002.

Salkin, Jeffrey K., ed. *The Modern Men's Torah Commentary: New Insights from Jewish Men on the 54 Weekly Torah Portions*. Woodstock, VT: Jewish Lights, 2009.

Schechter, S. *Studies in Judaism: First Series*. Philadelphia: Jewish Publication Society, 1911.

Scholem, Gershom. *Major Trends in Jewish Mysticism*. New York: Schocken Books, 1995.

———. *On the Kabbalah and Its Symbolism*. New York: Schocken Books, 1996.

———. *On the Mystical Shape of the Godhead: Basic Concepts in the Kabbalah*. New York: Schocken Books, 1997.

Shapiro, Marc B. *The Limits of Orthodox Theology: Maimonides' Thirteen Principles Reappraised*. Oxford: Littman Library, 2004.

Sherwin, Byron. *Studies in Jewish Theology: Reflections in the Mirror of Tradition*. London: Vallentine Mitchell, 2007.

———. *Faith Finding Meaning: A Theology of Judaism*. New York: Oxford University Press, 2009.

Soloveitchik, Joseph Dov. *Fate and Destiny: From Holocaust to the State of Israel*. Jersey City, NJ: KTAV, 2000.

———. *Halakhic Man*. Philadelphia: Jewish Publication Society, 1984.

———. *The Lonely Man of Faith*. 2nd ed. New York: Doubleday, 1992.

Spinoza, Baruch. *Theological-Political Treatise*. Translated by Samuel Shirley. Indianapolis: Hackett, 1998.

Steinberg, Milton. *Anatomy of Faith*. 1st ed. New York: Harcourt, Brace, 1960.

Steinberg, Milton, and Chaim Potok. *As a Driven Leaf*. Springfield, NJ: Behrman House, 1996.

Stone, Ira F. *Seeking the Path to Life: Theological Meditations on God and the Nature of People, Love, Life and Death*. Woodstock, VT: Jewish Lights, 1995.

Taylor, Charles. *Varieties of Religion Today: William James Revisited*. Cambridge: Harvard University Press, 2003.

Twersky, Isadore. *A Maimonides Reader*. Springfield, NJ: Behrman House, 1974.

Urbach, Ephraim. *The Sages*. Jerusalem: Magnes Press, 1979.

Walzer, Michael, et al., ed. *The Jewish Political Tradition: Volume 1—Authority*. New Haven: Yale University Press, 2000.

Wolf, Arnold Jacob, ed. *Rediscovering Judaism: Reflections on a New Theology*. Chicago: Quadrangle Books, 1965.

Wolpe, David J. *The Healer of Shattered Hearts: A Jewish View of God*. New York: Penguin, 1995.

———. *Why Faith Matters*. New York: HarperOne, 2009.

About Jewish Lights

People of all faiths and backgrounds yearn for books that attract, engage, educate, and spiritually inspire.

Our principal goal is to stimulate thought and help all people learn about who the Jewish People are, where they come from, and what the future can be made to hold. While people of our diverse Jewish heritage are the primary audience, our books speak to people in the Christian world as well and will broaden their understanding of Judaism and the roots of their own faith.

We bring to you authors who are at the forefront of spiritual thought and experience. While each has something different to say, they all say it in a voice that you can hear.

Our books are designed to welcome you and then to engage, stimulate, and inspire. We judge our success not only by whether or not our books are beautiful and commercially successful, but by whether or not they make a difference in your life.

For your information and convenience, at the back of this book we have provided a list of other Jewish Lights books you might find interesting and useful. They cover all the categories of your life:

Bar/Bat Mitzvah	Life Cycle
Bible Study / Midrash	Meditation
Children's Books	Men's Interest
Congregation Resources	Parenting
Current Events / History	Prayer / Ritual / Sacred Practice
Ecology / Environment	Social Justice
Fiction: Mystery, Science Fiction	Spirituality
Grief / Healing	Theology / Philosophy
Holidays / Holy Days	Travel
Inspiration	12-Step
Kabbalah / Mysticism / Enneagram	Women's Interest

RABBI ELLIOT J. COSGROVE, PHD, is rabbi at Park Avenue Synagogue in Manhattan. He received his masters of Hebrew letters from American Jewish University, studied at the Schechter Institute of Judaic Studies in Jerusalem, and was ordained at The Jewish Theological Seminary. He received his doctorate in the history of Judaism from the University of Chicago Divinity School.

RABBI DAVID J. WOLPE is rabbi of Sinai Temple in Los Angeles, and author of *Why Faith Matters,* among other books.

RABBI CAROLE B. BALIN, PHD, is professor of Jewish history at Hebrew Union College–Jewish Institute of Religion. She is currently working on an updated version of the 1984 edition of *Liberal Judaism* with Dr. Eugene B. Borowitz and Frances W. Schwartz.

"Masterfully assembled and beautifully presented … inspiring…. Brings together some of the most creative thinkers in the organized Jewish community today."
—*Tikkun*

"Could hardly be more timely."
—*Jewish Chronicle*

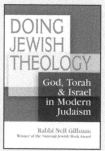 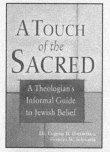 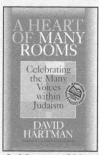

Printed in the USA
CPSIA information can be obtained
at www.ICGtesting.com
JSHW022327140824
68134JS00019B/1346